The Suff

GW00731444

The Korean Pentecost and The Sufferings Which Followed

WILLIAM NEWTON BLAIR
and
BRUCE F HUNT

The Banner of Truth Trust

THE BANNER OF TRUTH TRUST
3 Murrayfield Road, Edinburgh EH12 6EL
P.O. Box 621, Carlisle, Pennsylvania 17013, USA
© The Banner of Truth Trust 1977
First published 1977
ISBN 0 85151 244 5

Printed in Great Britain by
Hazell Watson & Viney Ltd,
Aylesbury, Bucks

Contents

Contents

List of Illustrations

List of Illustrations

Introduction

by
Bruce F. Hunt

THIS LITTLE BOOK BY DR WILLIAM N. BLAIR WAS first printed in 1910 by The Board of Foreign Missions of the Presbyterian Church in the U.S.A. 'For use of the Board and Missions'. At that time it bore the title 'The Korea Pentecost – And other Experiences on the Mission Field'.

Only the last three chapters, totalling nine pages, actually tell about what Dr Blair called the 'Korea Pentecost', more commonly known as 'the Korean Revival of 1907'.

Although I myself was only three-and-a-half years old at that time, certain impressions, which I personally trace back to the stirring events of 1907, are still with me. Growing up in Korea until I was sixteen, in the years following the revival, and then later, during my forty-eight years as a missionary among the Koreans, I have heard the revival of 1907 referred to by missionaries and Koreans alike as a great turning-point in the history of the Korean church. In other countries, too, I have often heard the Korean revival spoken of with almost mystical respect.

In some circles today we hear people saying 'we need revival', or 'we must pray for revival'. And almost every congregation in Korea today, regardless of denomination, has one or more 'revival meetings' a year. It is noteworthy that in Korea itself, and especially in a denomination (Presbyterian) the majority of whose missionaries have recognized the 1907 revival as having had a great influence on church growth, there has been so little of what in the

West is known as Pentecostalism. It is only in recent years that the 'tongues movement' and the emphasis on 'faith healing' have become popular in Korea.

This new edition of Dr Blair's eyewitness account of the beginning of the 1907 revival goes forth in the belief that it may still have a use not only for Boards and Missions but for all who are interested in true revival. It is made from Dr Blair's personal copy. I believe that the unaltered eye-witness account, written only three years after the event, will be found valuable to those who are interested in missions, and to those who are attempting to discover the origin and the results of what has been widely considered to be one of the great revivals.

Dr Blair was only twenty-five years old, fresh out of seminary, when he arrived in Korea with his bride in 1901. He had been on the field a little over five years when the revival began, and was one of the evening speakers at the Bible Conference where it broke. He and the Rev Graham Lee were the only missionaries present at the meeting which is regarded as the beginning of the revival. Of the two, Dr Blair, who spent more than forty-two years as a missionary in Korea, became the sole surviving *western* witness. He lived on to the ripe age of nearly 94.

When many people today are talking of and praying for revival, and staid Presbyterians, Methodists and Episcopalians are being impressed by the glossolalia (tongues) movement and masses attracted to reputed 'faith healers', it is interesting that so soon after the Korean revival Dr Blair should have felt it necessary to use forty-one pages to describe what *preceded* the revival and only nine pages to tell of the actual revival itself. It is also of interest that the ninety-year-old Protestant movement in Korea, which at-tributes much of its forward surge to the 1907 revival, has, until recently, been known more for its emphasis on prayer, Bible study, personal work, sacrificial giving and missionary activity rather than for mere emotionalism. It is also worth noting that out of such a movement has grown a Protestant constituency of some two and a half million adherents, in less than a century.

It would seem wise for any sincere student of missions and revivals especially to notice the words in Dr Blair's own introduction, written so soon after those emotion-filled events, explaining this proportionately large amount of space given to the things that *preceded* the revival. He says, 'At first I planned to write only of that great out-pouring of God's Spirit, but the events connected with that time were so dramatic and unusual that I feared they might be misunderstood without some account of the previous history of the Church from its beginning and some of my own experiences with the Korean Christians'.

Over the years, different explanations have been given for the rapid rise, vitality and phenomenal growth of the Korean church. It is important therefore, to notice that, sixty-nine years ago, Dr Blair, in his description of the revival, did not fail to recognize and to evaluate the political, economic and cultural conditions existing in Korea which God may have used in turning the people to himself.

But even more interesting in the light of mission practices which later became almost routine for missionary work in Korea, are Dr Blair's observations concerning the day-to-day, year-by-year application of the Biblical and Christ-centred principles, methods of work, and actual practices which preceded the revival.

This book is reproduced and sent forth today in the interest of true revival. Some plant, others water, but God gives the increase. 'So then neither is he that planteth any thing, neither he that watereth; but God that giveth the increase'. 'But all these worketh the one and the same Spirit, dividing to each one severally *even as He will*' (I Corinthians 3 : 7; 12 : 11).

January 1977

BRUCE HUNT
1624 Rockwell Road
Abington
Pa. 19001
U.S.A.

Part 1 : The Korean Pentecost and Other Experiences

William Newton Blair

During my year of furlough, I have found everywhere the greatest interest in the progress of the Gospel in Korea, and particularly a desire to know and understand the facts concerning the revival of 1907. To meet this desire, I have put into writing my own recollections of the revival. At first I planned to write only of that great outpouring of God's Spirit, but the events connected with that time were so dramatic and unusual that I feared they might be misunderstood without some account of the previous history of the Church from its beginning and some of my own experiences with the Korean Christians during the eight happy years I have lived and worked among them.

William Newton Blair, 1910.

THERE WERE SIX OF US WHO SAILED TOGETHER
from San Francisco for Korea in August, 1901, on a
Japanese ship, the *America Maru*, going out for the first
time as missionaries under the Board of Foreign Missions
of the Presbyterian Church in the United States of America. Like most who go a-sailing for the first time, we were
seasick the first day, but the second morning found the sea
calm and beautiful. We were sailing straight towards the
rim of a great, strange basin filled level full of blue-green,
solid-looking water that resisted the vessel and foamed for
miles along our track. We seemed to be much lower than
the distant horizon, sailing continually upward, never
reaching the top. There were many Japanese and Chinese
on the lower decks, both fore and aft. Most of them squat-
ted in the sunlight recovering from the night's seasickness.
A few had already spread their blankets in sheltered spots,
playing steadily for money with long, slender cards or with
dice.

Presently we discovered a man, seated apart from the
rest, dressed in the oddest costume I had ever seen. He
wore a long, loose coat of white silk with sleeves nearly a
foot wide. On his head was a shiny black hat with a stiff
rim of three or four inches and a high crown in the middle
like an undergrown opera hat. It was made, as we after-
wards learned, of closely woven horse hair, starched stiff
and glistening, and so transparent that one could make out
the shape of his peculiar hair dress with the knot of black

hair, stuck through with a white pin, running up under the
crown of the hat. From what we had read we knew he must
be a Korean and, going as we were to give our lives for
Korea, we were at once greatly interested and tried to talk
to him; but he knew little English and we no Korean, so we
made poor progress. The next day, however, we found a
Japanese on board who said he thought he could help us.
Going down together, we said what we wished to the
Korean and the Japanese gentleman wrote it out in those
mysterious characters that adorn a Chinese laundry shop,
the classical language of the Chinese, which the Chinese
and the Japanese and the Koreans all use in common as
Europe used to use Latin. As our Japanese friend wrote,
the Korean stood looking over his shoulder. Presently we
could see intelligence dawning in the man's face. He
stretched out his hand and took the pen and wrote back in
answer, 'My name is Whang. I am not a Christian, but I am
glad that you are going to Korea to help my people.'

Every day after that, Mr Whang came up on the upper
deck and taught us words out of the Korean language.
There were six of us, as I have said, in our party going to
Korea as missionaries: Mr E. H. Miller and Mr W. M.
Barrett, Miss Mattie Henry and Miss Mary Barrett, and
Mrs Blair and myself. How eager we were to begin, like
children just starting school, unable to realize the hercu-
lean task before us and hence courageous to begin. I have
a note book with nearly two hundred words in it which I
caught from the lips of Mr Whang. Many are incorrect,
some impossible of identification; nevertheless the book is
exceedingly precious, my first steps in the Korean language.

By and by we came to Japan, first to Yokohama and
then to Kobe. Here we changed steamers. Mr Whang went

one way and we another. I have never seen our friend again to this day and do no know whether he is a Christian or not; but I shall always be greatly indebted to him. For one thing, just before he went away, he came bringing each of us a motto written with his own hand, also a white silk handkerchief. We learned then and there, what I have ever since found to be true of the Koreans, that they are a loving, generous-hearted people, knowing, it seems to me, even before they have heard the words of the Master, that it is more blessed to give than it is to receive.

Our new boat was not an *America Maru*, and not even to be compared with the well-equipped ferry that connects Japan and Korea today. It was one of those little freighters that swarm along the coast of Japan and Korea, with a Japanese crew and captain and 'foreign chow' after a fashion.

For a day we sailed across the beautiful inland sea of Japan, with its background of pine-clad mountains and waterfalls and numberless islands, with great curved, carved roofs of temples rising out of black, mysterious forests. Villages, villages all the way with their myriad white-sailed fishing craft blocking the water front or flocking to and from the sea.

Finally we reached Shimonoseki, the last Japanese port, and at sunset turned our faces westward to cross the Korean Strait, the last stage of our journey. The Korean Strait is usually rough, like the English Channel. That night, how it stormed! We lay all night desperately sick, longing for the morning. At last morning came and a quieter sea told us we were nearing land. Weak and dizzy, we climbed to the deck and looked, and there before us were the hills of Korea, bare, brown, desolate, as hopeless-looking hills as I had ever seen, without a tree upon them,

K.P.—2

in marked contrast with the beautiful green of the Japan we had left behind. We could make out here and there on the hillsides white objects that looked in the distance like tombstones. 'No,' someone said, 'they are not tombstones, but Koreans cutting the brushwood and even the grass, and binding them in bundles to use as fuel in the open fireplaces underneath their houses.'

After breakfast we went ashore in a 'sam-pan' to Fusan, the port of Korea. Fusan was not then worthy to be called a city. It was just a collection of mud-walled, straw-thatched huts with here and there a tile-roofed house among them, all so low that one could stand in the street and put his hand on the roof of any one of them. It was hardly fair to speak of streets at all. Most of the highways were narrow alleys zigzagging in and out among the houses. The city had no sewerage whatever, the filth from the houses coming out in a slow-moving green stream into open gutters.

Many Koreans in the streets turned to stare as we passed by. A few of the men were clean, but most of them wore soiled white garments with dirty head-bands and dishevelled hair. The children, playing naked in the streets, fled screaming at our approach, and old women with faces wrinkled and tanned like leather hastened out of their houses to see what was the matter. Some, with frightened babies on their backs, did not stop to put on an overskirt over their padded trousers. Others wore short jackets that covered a part of the breast. Many came out without their jackets, just as they had been working in the kitchen; while the dogs wormed out of little square holes underneath the walls in bands and set up a frenzy of barking. Korean dogs strenuously object to Westerners. In all the years I have been in Korea I have been able to make friends with but one Korean dog and he appeared to have foreign blood in him. Even the heathen children in Pyengyang will come out and bow down before us with their pretty 'Pyeng-an ha-sim-neka?' ('Are you in peace?') but the dogs object to us just as violently as they did nine years ago. In the dead of the night, no matter how quietly I may try to slip through the village streets, the dogs will smell me out and arouse the village with their howling. The Koreans say that we foreigners have an offensive odour to which the dogs object. There, in Fusan, too, for the first time, we saw Korean pigs, those scavengers of Asiatic cities, with their long noses, thin backs, and bellies dragging on the ground. No wonder Moses forbade the children of Israel to eat the flesh of swine. We never care to eat pork in Korea.

It was still the month of August, the hot season of alter-nating rain and blistering sunshine, and the sun with all its noonday strength blazed down upon the rain-soaked ground until it fairly steamed, and the stench went up like a cloud from the city. Weakened by the night's seasickness, we could scarcely resist the impulse to return to our ship and go back to the beautiful America whence we had come. Then it was that we thanked God for the Korean gentleman we had met on the *America Maru*. We knew that all the Koreans were not as dirty and hopeless as the people we saw in Fusan, but somewhere back behind those barren mountains were men like Whang; so we took cour-age and journeyed on.

Today* there is a railroad from Fusan to Seoul, the capital, and on along the west coast as far as Wei Ju. This was yet to come in 1901. Leaving Fusan that evening, we

* Readers will recall from the Introduction that these words were first written in the early part of the 20th century. This should be borne in mind with similar statements.

proceeded around the southern coast of Korea on the same
Japanese ship that brought us over from Japan, and came
in the evening of the second day to Mok-po, a small port
on the southwest tip of the peninsula where the Southern
Presbyterians have a mission station. We went ashore in
the dark and could see little of the place by the dim light
that filtered through the paper windows. Passing through
the town, we crossed what seemed to be a great mud-flat
and came to Dr Owen's house. How good it was to see an
American home again and the light streaming through
glass windows. Dr Owen gave us a true 'southern' welcome
and took us to see the Korean Church, a building in native
style about twenty feet by forty feet, with white paper on
the walls and clean mats on the floor, a curtain dividing
the room in two sections. It was prayer meeting evening
and about twenty men were seated on one side and about
twenty women on the other, not dressed in soiled garments
like the Koreans we had seen in Fusan, but clothed in spot-
less white. Someone was praying as we entered, and they
had all fallen forward until their foreheads rested rever-
entially on the mat floor in true Oriental fashion.

After the prayer Dr Owen told them who we were and
it broke up the meeting. They all crowded forward, eager
to tell us how glad they were that we had come so great a
distance to help the Korean people. I shall never forget
one old mother, who took both of my hands in hers and
poured a stream of meaningless words into my ear; but the
tears in her eyes and the love in her face needed no interpretation. We often know a Christian man from a heathen,
even before he speaks, by his changed countenance. We
never have any difficulty in recognizing a Christian old
woman. All her life long she has been in ignorance and
virtual bondage, scarcely as valuable to her husband as

the ox that plows his field, rising in the dark to cook the meals for her lord and master, eating whatever remains, after he has finished, toiling, often with a baby on her back, not only in the house, but frequently in the field with the men. Unwelcomed at birth, unloved through life, and with no hope of a better world beyond, she lives continually in fear of the demons that populate earth and sky; afraid to live and still more afraid to die. When to such an old Korean woman, just about to pass out into the unknown terrors beyond, comes the message of God's love and forgiveness and of a home in heaven, and she understands enough to know that God loves her and gave His Son in her stead, all the glory of it fills her soul to overflowing. It shines forth like sunshine, beautifying her old face with the love of Jesus.

That night at Mok-po, when the Korean Christians gathered around us in welcome, the dread and feeling of strangeness, the impossibility of getting behind the mask that masks an Oriental's feelings, all fell away in a moment, and I have always felt since then that I was just as close to a Korean Christian as to an American brother.

2 : Korea's Preparation for the Gospel

FROM MOK-PO WE JOURNEYED NORTH ALONG THE west coast, in and out among the thousands of islands that form the Korean Archipelago. The west coast, in marked contrast with the forbidding eastern coast, is very beautiful. Some of the islands are large, with villages in sheltered valleys; nearly all are wooded and bright with flowers. The mountains in the western half of the peninsula are low, with wide, fertile valleys between them, and many rivers flowing into the Yellow Sea.

Korea is about 600 miles long and 150 miles wide, lying between the thirty-third and forty-third parallels, about the same latitude as the central portion of the United States. In the north the climate is cold with two feet of snow on the ground all winter. The south is like that of southern Japan, semi-tropical with bamboo thickets.

The country abounds in small game, with deer and black bear in the north and wild boar, leopards and a few tigers in the central and southern parts. Nearly all the grains and fruits of America are found in Korea. Wheat, cane, corn, barley, millet, buckwheat, tobacco, ginseng, cotton, beans, potatoes and melons all do well; but the staple is rice. Apples, pears, peaches, plums, grapes, cherries, persimmons and berries of all sorts are easily grown; but the native varieties are usually of poor quality, except persimmons, which are exceptionally fine. The difficulty in the past of protecting fruit from thieves greatly hindered its culture. Korea is naturally a fruit country, and some day her hills will be covered with orchards and vineyards.

The Korean people resemble the Chinese and Japanese in appearance, but are distinct from both these nations. Their language, though containing many Chinese derivatives, is a separate root language, difficult to master, but sweet and musical to the ear. Korea has a fairly reliable history running back over three thousand years, while uncertain myths carry it still further back in time.

The Koreans are naturally a poetic, deeply-religious people. They love to study and ponder the wise sayings of the sages. Even the humble homes of the farmers often have classical quotations written on walls and doorposts. A surprisingly large proportion of the people can read and write not only their own language, but the classical language of the Chinese as well.

Although Confucianism originated in China, the Koreans have out-Chinesed the Chinese in practising some of its precepts. The essence of Confucianism is reverence for established authority and order, above all, that the son should honour his father. To the literal-minded Korean this meant that he should not dishonour the past by attempting to improve upon it. Men have been put to death in Korea for daring to make some new invention. Gripped by this dominant religious idea, Korea stood stock-still amidst the current of the centuries, while China, in spite of herself, moved slowly on until she was modern as compared with Korea. I have seen images in ancient Chinese temples with the same topknot and general style of clothing that the Koreans wear today, proving that centuries ago the Chinese and Korean customs were similar. It is not necessarily a sign of weakness for a nation to stand still as Korea has done. The forces of progress are well nigh irresistible. Only a strong religious conviction and an ability to realize in practice the creed she professed enabled Korea to remain immovable for three thousand years.

Buddhism came to Korea from India by way of China in the fourth century of the Christian era. It contained much that was a distinct advance over the old Animism. Confucianism taught right conduct as an ethical system, Buddhism sought to enforce it by religious authority. Its priests announced a heaven for saints and a fearful hell for sinners. A door of communion with the spirit-world was opened up. Prayer and sacrifice, it was claimed, were the keys that unlocked the doors of the inner temple where forgiveness might be found, and peace enjoyed forever. As she has always done, when once her trust was won, Korea entered into Buddhism whole-heartedly. She dotted her hills with Buddhist temples and gave rich lands as their endowment. Korean Buddhist priests crossed over the sea to Japan and converted the Japanese to Buddhism. It was not a military but a spiritual conquest, won as such conquests are usually won, by martyrs' blood and irresistible devotion.

Now we come to a special instance of God's providence. Buddhism is dead in Korea. Go to China and you will find the temples in good repair, go to Japan and in every village you will find the temples flourishing, their roofs looming high above the houses. You will hear the tinkle, tinkle of the bells and see the multitudes pressing through the gates and bowing down before tablets of wood and idols of stone, just as blind as ever. In Korea it is not so. The temples are there, but they are falling and in ruins. There are holes in the tiled roofs where the bats make their homes, where the rainy season floods come through and rot the wooden pillars. The people despise the few shaven-headed priests who remain. The fact is, Confucianism killed Buddhism in Korea. After the first enthusiasm had passed away and the Buddhist Church had become rich and powerful, the priests grew corrupt and arrogant. Their lazy, immoral lives disgusted the Korean people, schooled as they were in the high ethics of Confucius, and when the Buddhist hierarchy sought to interfere with the affairs of state, the government itself turned upon Buddhism and gave it its death blow. Most of the temple lands were taken away and the priests forbidden to enter the capital city. Today they point a finger of scorn at a Buddhist priest, calling him a 'nom,' a 'low down scoundrel.'

So we find a remarkable state of things in Korea, a people by nature intensely religious without any entrenched religion with priests able to hinder the progress of Christianity. Confucianism, considered apart from ancestral worship, which has been added on, is not a religion. It is the far eastern world's system of morals, the schoolmaster, if you please, that is today leading Korea to the feet of Christ.

One other condition that must be noticed in any consideration of the remarkable progress of the gospel in Korea in the 20th century is her preparation of suffering and humiliation. The location of Korea creates difficulties. Lying midway between China and Japan she has been for thousands of years a bone of contention between these two nations, both claiming suzerainty over her. First China would demand and compel tribute, then Japan would pour her warriors across the channel and punish the Koreans for yielding to China. When these two nations have had no quarrel with Korea they have usually been at war with each other and have fought out their quarrels on the long suffering soil of Korea until the land has run with blood again and again. As a consequence the people, unable to resist the hordes that came upon them, built cities of refuge high in the mountains, where they might flee when one by one their walled cities fell before the ruthless invaders. It is a mistake to suppose that the Korean people are a cowardly people. Their history is replete with records of heroism and desperate bravery in defence of home and country. They have simply been overpowered. The marvel is that in spite of all they have suffered, they remain unbroken and an integral people with one language and one blood, numbering today fully thirteen million.

No wonder Korea is poor. Not only has she been continually devastated by war, but her own government has often been worthless and rotten. For centuries her kings 'farmed out' the rule to magistrates and governors who paid many times their salary for the office, and then squeezed back the amount and many times more from the people by unjust methods. It has been as much as a man's life was worth for it to become known that he had accumulated anything, unless he had powerful friends to protect him. If the robbers neglected to come down from the mountains and take it away, the robber magistrate would send out his 'runners,' arrest a man on some trumped-up charge, throw him into prison and beat him till he would be glad to pay all that he had for his life.

Recently the greatest misfortune of all, at least in Korean eyes, befell their country. After the Russo-Japanese war of 1904, the Japanese withdrew a large part of their victorious army from Manchuria back into Korea. Japanese soldiers were posted in every city and hamlet. The few Korean troops were forcibly disbanded and the common people compelled to give up their guns. Even the old flint-lock guns that the mountaineers used for tiger hunting were collected and burned in heaps, where I have seen the mass of their tangled barrels lying. A treaty was secured from the Korean government giving Japan absolute control of Korea's foreign affairs and virtual control of the internal administration.

It is easy enough for an outsider to look on and philosophically remark that it was inevitable that either Russia or Japan must prevail, and better Japan than Russia. It is not so easy for the sufferer to see God's hand in the malady. I have no political purpose in writing this narrative and am merely trying to show conditions and how these conditions have conspired in God's providence to work out salvation for Korea. The simple truth is that the Koreans are a broken-hearted people. Corrupt and unworthy as their old government was, nevertheless they loved it, and all the more, no doubt, in proportion as it seems to be taken away from them. It is pitiable to see them grieve, to see strong men weep over national loss. They come to us and say, 'Is there any country so poor, so unfortunate as ours?' But it means much that their eyes are open. Formerly they were proud and arrogant; they were 'wretched and miserable and poor and blind and naked,' and knew it not. Now, with respect to this world, at least, they know just where they stand. They know they are despised and rejected. The arrow had entered Korea's soul. Her spirit was broken. For years now she has been sitting in the dust, mourning not only her present misfortunes, but her past sins. Over just such a stricken people has God so often stretched out his hands in blessing. By brokenness of spirit Korea has been prepared for the Gospel, and when a further work of God's Spirit was manifested the Scripture was again fulfilled: 'The sacrifices of God are a broken spirit; a broken and a contrite heart, O God, thou wilt not despise.'

3 : How the Gospel Came to North Korea

IN THE SUMMER OF THE YEAR 1832 THE FIRST
Protestant missionary visited Korea. He was Charles Gützlaff. Born in Pomerania and educated at Halle, the centre
of the German pietistic movement in the seventeenth century, Gützlaff served first at Batavia and then in Bangkok,
Siam. Later he moved to Macao, where he became an intimate friend of Robert Morrison, the first Protestant missionary to China. In 1832 the East India Company sent
Charles Gützlaff and H. H. Lindsay to the northern ports
of China, in the ship *Amherst*, in order to discover how
far these ports might be gradually opened to British trade,
and to what extent the disposition of the natives and the
local government would be favourable to it. Robert Morrison sent a large stock of Chinese Scriptures to Gützlaff
for distribution during his voyage. After visiting the Shantung coasts, the ship sailed for Korea. At first it anchored
near the Cape of Changsan, on the west coast of Whanghae
Province. The explorers made an attempt to reach the
court by a letter through the local magistrates, but their
efforts failed. They resumed their voyage toward the south
and reached the west coast of the Ch'ung Ch'yong Province. While the *Amherst* was anchored at Basil's Bay, a
petition, together with presents, was despatched to the
king, through the local officials, requesting an opening of
commercial intercourse. While they were waiting for the
reply from the capital, the visitors came into contact with
the people. Gützlaff distributed Bibles and religious tracts,

and planted potatoes. The petition and the presents, after a long delay, were returned. The visitors were informed that Korea could not permit them to trade without first consulting China.

Gützlaff reports: 'According to all accounts which we could collect, there are at present no Europeans at the capital, and Christianity is unknown, even by name.' Before he went to Korea, Gützlaff had known the 'detailed accounts of persecution' of Catholicism in Korea, but he 'could discover no trace of it.'

Gützlaff's visit to Korea was so brief that no recognisable result was produced. But the first Protestant missionary to visit the peninsula spoke of his visit with unshaken faith: 'At all events it is the work of God, which I frequently commended in my prayers to his gracious care. Can the divine truth, disseminated in Korea be lost? This I believe not: there will be some fruits in the appointed time of the Lord. In the great plan of the eternal God, there will be a time of merciful visitation for them. While we look for this we ought to be very anxious to hasten its approach, by diffusing the glorious doctrines of the cross by all means and power . . . The Scripture teaches us to believe that God can bless even these feeble beginnings. Let us hope that better days will soon dawn for Korea.' But no Protestant missionary was to visit Korea for the next thirty-three years, until the long silence of the gospel was broken by R. J. Thomas.*

Rev Robert J. Thomas was born in Wales, September 7, 1840. He went to China in 1863 as an agent of the London Missionary Society. In 1865, he met two Koreans,

* This information about Gützlaff is here added to Dr Blair's account and is drawn from G. L. Paik, *The History of Protestant Missions in Korea, 1832–1910* (1927).

members of the Catholic Church in Chefoo, in the home of
Rev A. Williamson, of the National Bible Society of Scot-
land. When Mr Thomas found that these Koreans could
read the Chinese Scriptures and learned from them that all
educated Koreans could read the Chinese characters, he
resolved then and there to go to Korea and give the Korean
people the Gospel in Chinese. This was a resolution easier
to make than to carry out as Korea was then a hermit
country forbidding all foreigners on the pain of death from
entering her borders. But Mr Thomas never wavered in
his determination to go to Korea.

In September of 1865 he secured a vessel with financial
help from Mr Williamson, and succeeded in reaching
islands near the west coast of Korea.

Unable to reach the mainland of Korea, Mr Thomas returned to China only to make a second attempt one year
later when he found that an American owned ship called
The General Sherman planned to make a voyage of ex-
ploration to Korea. No doubt the officers of the ship
hesitated to permit a missionary to accompany them on
such a dangerous journey, but somehow they were persu-
aded to receive Mr Thomas and his cargo of Gospel tracts
and Bibles. On board the ship were five Occidentals: Mr
Preston, the owner; Mr Page, the Master; Mr Wilson, the
Mate; an Englishman named Hogart and Mr Thomas and
a crew of 24 Chinese and Malays.

The General Sherman crossed the Yellow Sea and entering the mouth of the Tai Tong River sailed slowly up this
wide river towards the walled city of Pyengyang on the
west bank of the Tai Tong River fifty miles inland. Stops
were made at several places and at each place Mr Thomas
gave copies of the Scriptures to those bold enough to receive them and left other copies on the bank of the river.

Nearing Pyengyang the officers of the ship went ashore and met the governor of Pyengyang and the commander of the garrison who seemed disposed to be friendly. Unfortunately the crew of *The General Sherman* detained five Koreans on board ship when they resumed the journey toward Pyengyang. This greatly frightened the captured men and enraged the Korean people, especially when two of the captured men were drowned trying to escape from the foreign vessel. Rumours spread that the foreigners had come to rob the ancient tombs and to secure eyes of little children for foreign medicine.

There are a number of islands in the river just below Pyengyang City with swift rapids above and below them. Only once a month at high tide is it possible for an ocean-going vessel to ascend these rapids. It so happened that *The General Sherman* arrived at the full of the moon and passed over the rapids without difficulty and anchored above the islands in sight of the walled city.

Thousands of Koreans lined the banks on both sides of the river, shouting and discharging their flintlock guns at the unwelcome visitors. Little damage was done, but no landing was possible. After several days of this sort of thing the men on *The General Sherman* decided in favour of discretion as the better part of valour. But they had waited too long. When they started to descend the river their ship went aground in the middle of the first rapid and could not be dislodged. Even here they were able to keep the Koreans at a distance with their superior arms for a number of days. During this time at least twenty Koreans were killed and many more injured. In the meantime the Koreans secured a large number of small fishing boats and piled them high with dry pine branches. Binding them together with iron chains they stretched them out in a long line across the river. Then at the right moment, when the tide was running swiftly towards the ocean, they set the boats all on fire and let them drift like outstretched arms of flame down the river to encircle *The General Sherman*. With their ship on fire the men on board had no alternative but to plunge into the water and make for the shore where the Koreans waited for them with knives and clubs and rifles.

All of the foreigners were killed, but there was a difference. The Koreans say that the men from *The General Sherman* came out of the water armed with swords and pistols and tried to defend themselves; all save one who acted very strangely. This man staggered out of the water with his arms full of books which he thrust into the hands of the Koreans as they clubbed him down.

Of course they killed Mr Thomas, not knowing that he had come to Korea to help them; not knowing the precious gift he offered. But multitudes in Korea know today that the Bible is the most precious book in the world and God has marvellously kept His promise, 'My word shall not return to me void.' Though the officials in Pyengyang sought to gather and burn all the Bibles which Mr Thomas left at various places along the river, and tossed to the crowd as he died at the river's edge, many copies were concealed and read later in secret. One of the early catechumens received by Dr Moffett in Pyengyang some twenty-seven years later was the son of a man who had received one of these Bibles. In Pyengyang City today* there are twenty-seven Presbyterian Churches with an attendance of over ten thousand besides many churches of other denominations. All down the Tai Tong River strong churches mark the places where Mr Thomas gave the gospel to Korea and across the river just below Pyengyang stands the

* 1957.

beautiful Thomas Memorial Chapel which the Presbyterian Church of Korea has erected in gratitude to God for the man who gave his life for Korea.

IT IS A SIGNIFICANT FACT THAT TWO GREAT American Churches, the Methodist and Presbyterian, were led to begin work in Korea at about the same time, and that largely upon these churches and the reinforcements that have come from the American Methodist Church South, the American Southern Presbyterian Church, and the Canadian and Australian Presbyterian Churches, has fallen the great burden and privilege of bringing Korea to Christ.

The pioneers on the Presbyterian side were Dr Horace N. Allen, Rev Horace G. Underwood, D.D., and Dr J. W. Heron, and on the Methodist side, Dr William B. Scranton and Rev Harry G. Appenzeller. They were quickly followed by many others. God's blessing attended the work from the beginning; but the great awakening began in Pyengyang, the ancient capital of Korea, beautifully located on the west bank of the Tai Tong River, about two hundred miles north of Seoul, the present capital.

Several missionaries had early visited Pyengyang, but it was not till 1893 that Rev Samuel A. Moffett of the Presbyterian Church and Dr W. J. Hall of the Methodist Church actually established residences in the city. It was not my privilege to know Dr Hall personally as he died in 1895, but his memory is fragrant in Pyengyang. The Koreans still love to tell of his sweet character and zeal in proclaiming the Master.

To Dr Moffett fell the great privilege and honour not

only to be the founder of the Pyengyang Church, but for seventeen years to be its guiding spirit and beloved leader. He had the rare ability of uniting men, not so much about himself, as in the common service. God gifted him with wisdom and insight into the future to such a degree that the Koreans frequently allude to him as a 'sun-che-cha' ('prophet'). He was still a young man, with light hair and grey-blue eyes, when I went to Pyengyang, little changed, I fancy, from the day he first entered the city. Stories are still current of the excitement produced. The rumour spread like wildfire that a crazy foreigner had come to live in Pyengyang. Wonderful tales were told of his height, of his narrow trousers, of his white eyes and white hair and great beak of a nose. The Koreans wear huge trousers; they have jet black hair and eyes and think all foreigners have enormous noses. Just as people crowd to a circus in America, they crowded to see Dr Moffett, till they blocked the road in front of his house so that the ox-carts could not go by. We are no longer objects of great curiosity in Pyengyang, but out in the country districts it is still common to have one's room besieged. We grow hardened, I suppose, and cease to mind very much except at meal time. Then I always request my boy to shut the paper door and window of my room. Frequently, however, if I look up suddenly from my position on the floor in front of the little table on which my meal has been served, I will find that several boys, perhaps men, have come silently to the outside, and pressing moist fingers to the paper window, have punctured holes and are staring down at me like the eyes of disembodied spirits. It gives a man a queer, creepy sort of feeling down his back. During my seminary days, I used to enjoy going to Lincoln Park and watching the keepers feed the animals. Since going to Korea, I have often felt like apologizing to the animals.

Among those who came to see Dr Moffett was a stalwart Korean named Chai Cho-si, who kept a saloon in the city, with a blue flag split down the middle to show that he had liquor to sell. This man came many times, no doubt to get a good story to tell to the loafers in his saloon. In some way the missionary's story got hold of him and he understood enough of it to do what we say in Korea, 'Yasu mit-ki-rul chak-chung hasso' – beautiful words they are – 'he decided to believe in Jesus.' This man became a strong right arm to Dr Moffett. He closed his saloon and gave much time to spreading the new doctrine. Almost before they knew it there was a church in Pyengyang, a company of men and women professing the name of Jesus, assembling for worship on the Lord's Day. Then the magistrate heard of it. 'Ah,' he said, 'you can't do that here. If you worship according to the foreigners' religion, how are you going to worship the spirits of your ancestors at the New Year's time.' This is the great cross of the Korean Church. Each New Year every son of Korea must bow before the tablets that represent to him the spirits of his dead ancestors. Not to bow down, not to offer the yearly sacrifice, is to be guilty of the greatest sin possible in Korea, namely, filial impiety. But Christianity has never been able to compromise with idols. The Church has had to show that men can honour parents without idolatry.

The magistrate sent out his runners and arrested the Christians. Some were beaten, some were threatened with death. A mob hurled stones at the missionary as he walked through the streets. No one knows just what would have happened if, at that juncture, there had not come down from the north the Chinese behind their yellow dragon banners. Up from the south came the Japanese, new armed with modern rifles, and the Japanese–Chinese war was on (1894). The two armies met in Pyengyang. The little company of Christians was scattered like sheep to the mountains, as the early Christians were scattered at the time of the great persecution in Jerusalem, and like those early Christians they went everywhere preaching the gospel.

Dr Moffett was given official instructions to return to Seoul, the capital. As soon as possible after the battle at Pyengyang, he went back bringing several others with him. They found the city burned to the ground, with the bodies of dead Chinamen lying unburied in the streets. Soon word went out to the surrounding country that the missionaries had returned and the Christians began to gather back, bringing wonderful tidings of little groups of Christians springing up all over the northland. God's Spirit had been using those days of war and peril to make men welcome the message of His love and the comfort of the gospel. Have you ever seen a fire smouldering in the ashes on a still day? Suddenly a little whirlwind comes down, lifts up the embers, and scatters them all around, so that here and there and yonder other fires begin burning. This is just what happened in Korea. There was a fire God's Spirit had kindled, burning in Pyengyang. Suddenly the whirlwind of the war came down and lifted up and scattered the fire for hundreds of miles in every direction and everywhere those living embers fell, whether on level rice plains near the sea, or in deep-set mountain valleys, other fires began to blaze and spread until the fire of the gospel was burning throughout the whole length and breadth of the peninsula.

Reinforcements were hurried to Pyengyang. Every effort was made to conserve the work, to visit each new group of believers. The missionaries made long trips into the country in every direction, organizing and instructing the new converts. But in spite of all they could do, though they lived among the Koreans till their own children failed to recognize them, though they travelled day and night, the work travelled faster. Overwhelmed, they sent out a great Macedonian cry that began to ring north and south in the United States of America, 'Come over and help us!'

One of the Pyengyang missionaries, Rev W. L. Swallen, came to America and to Chicago in 1901, when I was a senior in McCormick Seminary. One Monday night he addressed the students and pleaded as a man pleads for his life, for some of us to go out and preach the Word in Korea. 'Ah,' I said, 'that is a great story, but I could never learn that language.' I had never enjoyed language work in either college or seminary. 'Surely,' I reasoned, 'if God wanted me to go to the foreign field he would have given me more facility in language.' So I hardened my heart. That night, about the midnight hour, Mr Swallen came to my room. It was not till nine years later that I learned who told him about me. 'Blair,' he said, 'why don't you go to Korea? Don't you know we need you?' 'Why, Mr Swallen,' I answered, 'as far as the hardships and all that go, I think they would rather appeal to me; but that language, I could never learn that language.' 'Are you honest?' he questioned. 'Is that the reason you don't volunteer?' 'Yes,' I said, 'I think I am.' 'Well,' he said, 'Let me tell something. When I was here in the Seminary, I flunked* in Hebrew. Have you flunked in Hebrew?' If ever in my life I wished that I might tell a man that I had flunked in anything it was that night; but I had not actually flunked in Hebrew and had to admit it. Here was a man who said he had trouble in languages and yet God had enabled him to get the Korean language. So I found I could not excuse

* Flunk = to fail, and back out (American college slang).

myself on that score any longer. After considerable de-
liberation, I wrote a letter to the young lady out in Kansas
who had promised to share life's problems with me, saying
that I was ready to volunteer if she was willing to go, half
hoping, I am afraid, that she would say 'No'. Her answer
was this: 'I am so glad. I hoped you would volunteer.' So
I sent my name to the Board of Foreign Missions and was
accepted and went out to Korea, as I have already described in the opening chapter, going out a good deal like a
drafted soldier, but I will never, never get through thank-
ing the good Lord that I did go, just when I did, when I was
so needed, in time to share in the great Pentecostal movement that came as the blessing of heaven.

WE ARRIVED IN SEOUL, KOREA, SEPTEMBER 12, 1901, and after a month of various mission meetings went to Pyengyang where we had been stationed. Of course our first task was to get the language. If I had known how hard and how long a task it would be, I am afraid I would have been more frightened even than I was when in Chicago. It is one of those old Oriental languages overburdened with words and endless endings. Euphony is its main law. All the words are softened to harmonize with their fellows. Each is dovetailed into the next till it is scarcely possible to tell where one word ends and another commences. It pours forth in a steady stream, a smoothly-flowing uphill-and-downhill sort of language. Sometimes I would make the most ridiculous mistakes. Chopping a word right in the middle and joining it with half the next, I would go to some Korean and ask him what it meant. 'Morogesso' ('I don't know'), he would say, and of course he did not, for no Korean ever uttered such a combination.

I was almost in despair when one Sunday after a service a slight, clean-featured man named Ne Che-su came to me and said something that I could not understand, but I could discern a distinction in the sounds he uttered. At my suggestion, one of the missionaries asked Mr Ne to become my teacher and he consented. I well remember the first words he taught me. I was seated at my desk ready to begin; but he was not. 'Kedo-hapsata,' he said, and I understood him, for in a moment he had slipped from his place by my side to the floor and was praying. 'Kedo-hapsata' ('Let's pray'), and every morning and afternoon for three years it was 'Kedo-hapsata.' God sent me a Spirit-filled teacher and he prayed the language into me, prayed and laboured until I became afraid not to study as hard as I ought. Sometimes when I was dull of comprehension, he would act out the meaning. Once he got down on the floor and wrapped himself up in the carpet in a desperate effort to make me understand the word 'chanda' ('I sleep'). I have come to believe in the gift of tongues, not a sudden, miraculous ability to speak an unknown language. That would not be well for us nor for the people to whom we go. We are ignorant of their customs and dispositions. Our tempers are too unruly and our tongues too swift. Dumbness at first is a blessing to all concerned. But that God does keep His promise, that He gives strength and patience and to our great surprise even pleasure in studying the language, I know. Little by little our ears are unstopped and the tightly tied strings of our tongues are loosened, till almost before we know it, as a child begins to prattle its mother's tongue, we begin to speak the language of the people about us. I want to say here for the encouragement of any who may be hesitating as I was, that it is not so much a question of special gift in language or of a remarkable memory, as of a fairly good ear and a willingness to work and live among the people.

As soon as I could speak enough Korean to begin preaching, five counties were assigned to my care north of Pyengyang City, partly mountainous and partly level rice plains along the Yellow Sea. At first the church work was small and I had leisure to preach to the people as I walked the roads. There are few good roads in Korea. For the most part there are only crooked paths that seek the lowest passes in the mountains and wind in and out between the rice fields. Most Koreans walk. That seemed too slow for me, so I got a nice, red bicycle from Chicago, but I soon gave it up. I met too many men leading enormous oxen, loaded down with brushwood till they looked like moving wood piles with horns in front and tails behind. You can imagine what a great country ox like that would do if he met a foreigner in a narrow path on a bicycle. Conditions have changed greatly in Korea during the last few years. We now have a railroad running the length of the land. I am even planning to take out a motorcycle to Korea to use on long journeys. Nevertheless, I mean to walk as much as possible because it is the best way to preach the gospel. Jesus walked, and much of Korea today is still much like Palestine was in the days of Christ.

I enjoy walking with my Korean friends, filling my lungs with the fresh mountain air, jumping streams without bridges, throwing bits of rock at impudent magpies. If it is a long pull up a mountain, how delicious to sit awhile on the summit and rest, and look back over the trail far below, to see the villages nestling like flocks of quails at the base of the mountains, to see the tiny streamlets winding like silver ribbons among the rice fields. To the north and south and east, as far as the eye can see, are mountains behind mountains, forest peaks of mountains, till the grey of the mountains is lost in the blue of the sky. To the west lie a few scattered mountains with broad valleys between, and in the distance the long line of the Yellow Sea, with the smoke of a steamer or the white sails of junks going across to China. In walking one has time to talk over the work together, to plan evening meetings, to discuss endless problems.

There is a system of market in Korea, five towns in a

circle. The market town may not have more than twenty houses; but every fifth day it blossoms into a full-grown city, a great beehive of peddlers with their wares spread out on mats along the road, and farmers from miles in every direction. There are no fixed prices. It is a regular Jews' market. Everybody shouts at the top of his lungs to be heard above the din. What seems to be a fight is probably only a prelude to a bargain, a friendly contest of wind and wits between two old bluffers. A market is a fine place to meet men and an excellent spot in which to preach the gospel.

Frequently we will overtake a crowd of farmers going to market, a woman with a bundle of cloth on her head, a boy leading a donkey laden with rice, perhaps a man with firewood piled high on his back on a wooden frame called a 'jickey,' or he may have eggs in strings heaped high above his back like cordwood. They put ten eggs in a string, placed end to end, and bound with rice straw till you can grasp one end and hold the string out like a poker. We may meet a man with a pig on his back, its four feet tied together and its snout bound so that it cannot interrupt a conversation. A strange sight, but he moves along just as innocently as can be.

They smile at me and I at them. No one has any business to be on the foreign field if he lacks a sense of humour. Presently, someone will hear me speak. 'What, can the foreigner speak our language?' he exclaims. 'Oh, yes,' one of my friends will answer, 'he speaks it very well.' The Koreans are exceedingly polite and great flatterers, at least in your presence. By and by, I introduce myself to the nearest man. No third party is necessary, etiquette prescribing certain set phrases to use in introduction. I generally begin by asking the man where he is going, then where

he lives. He probably answers, 'Over behind that mountain,' and asks me where I live, and I tell him, 'Outside the
West Gate at Pyengyang.' Then I ask him about the price
of eggs and chickens, and we discuss the crops and the
weather. Finally, I ask the question that I have come from
America to ask, 'Have you heard the story of Jesus?' Very
likely he answers, 'I know a little, but not clearly.' Then I
begin away back with how God made the world for man's
benefit, and filled it with fruit and flowers and all that he
needed for his good, how men everywhere turned their
backs upon the good God and bowed themselves down to
tablets of wood and idols of stone, and got to themselves
thereby terrible hurt and damage; how sickness and sorrow, suffering and death resulted. I tell how God so loved
the world that He sent His Son from heaven and Jesus was
born, not in the United States of America, but in Bethle-
hem of Judea, down southwest of China. It makes a world
of difference to an Oriental to know that Jesus was born
in Asia. I tell of His life and His love, and at last of His
death on the cross. I know I never understood half the
meaning of the crucifixion till I stood by the wayside in
Korea, forgetting to go on, and showed a Korean who had
never heard the story before, how they pierced His feet and
drove nails into His hands. Then I heard the man say,
'Aigo, kurus-sim-nika?' ('Oh, my, is that true?'). From
such wayside meetings we would sometimes see a new face
in church the next Sunday.

In those early days, there were few good places in which
to sleep at night, so we frequently stayed at public inns. The
inn is usually an ordinary Korean house, consisting of a
living-room sixteen to twenty feet long and eight feet wide.
A kitchen is found at one end, with a dirt floor dug out a
foot below the level of the ground in order that the flames

and smoke from the fireplace, over which the innkeeper's wife cooks the rice for her guests in a huge iron kettle, can pass underneath the stone-slabbed floor of the living-room by a system of flues cut in the ground, and out of a high chimney at the farther end. Mud mixed with finely chopped rice-straw is plastered over the stone floor. At first the heat cracks the mud, but after being washed a few times with a wet broom the whole floor bakes hard and smooth like the floor of an oven. The room is generally quite bare of furniture except for a mat on the floor, a box on one side where the bedquilts are kept by day, and two earthen vessels at the upper end of the room half full of liquor.

Usually there are probably three to ten guests ahead of us, already stretched out on the warm floor, or sitting cross-legged, puffing away at their long tobacco pipes, till the room is choked with smoke. In winter, no matter how many people occupy the room, all the doors and windows are kept tightly shut to conserve the heat in the stone floor. Scientists tell us wonderful stories about how many cubic yards of fresh air a man must have to exist. It is evidently not so, at least in Korea.

Whenever possible, I bribe the innkeeper for the hire of a small inner room. Sometimes I have recklessly paid as much as ten cents to get him to send his wife and children to the neighbours to obtain these private quarters; but frequently bribery fails, or there is no inner room, and I have to share the front room with the family and the public. Every good traveller is prepared for such an emergency. We usually take a pack-pony with us, loading him down with two wooden boxes about the size of cracker-boxes, and tied firmly one on either side of the wooden pack-saddle. One of the boxes contains canned goods and cooking utensils for the journey, and the other, books and clothing. On top of the boxes is placed a large bag, called a 'tarrion,' packed with bed-clothing, and on top of the 'tarrion,' the most wonderful thing a missionary possesses, his folding army-cot. I generally carry a rubber blanket to protect the load from rain, and then the pack is complete.

When I have to sleep in a public inn, I first unfold the cot, to the unbounded astonishment of the Koreans, and place it crosswise across the room, just as close as possible to the whiskey barrels, not because I particularly admire the whiskey barrels, but because the Koreans prefer the lower, hotter part of the room and I decidedly do not. Then my rubber blanket is hung up to form a partition across the room and I am ready to sleep. Not quite, however. When the lights are out, I rise and stealthily cut a slit down the paper window about a foot long and two inches wide. This is what habit does for a man. I could not possibly sleep in that air-tight room with all those Koreans. The next morning a few pennies will more than compensate the owner.

Most Korean inns are also livery stables, with a long shed to the rear where the horses and donkeys are fed bean soup in a long log trough with hollowed out sections. Long after I have gone to bed I can hear them fussing with their horses. Each animal is settled for the night by having a rope passed under its belly and securely fastened to a strong beam overhead. A unique device to save currying! There they swing on tiptoe in a long row, half standing, half hanging, all the night through; restlessly jingling the bells under their necks, and at intervals breaking loose and arousing the neighbourhood with their kicking and squealing. Needless to say, an inn is a poor place for slumber.

6 : Caring for the Churches

NOWADAYS WE RARELY SLEEP IN INNS. THE CHURCH work has grown until there are now more than forty church buildings in my five counties. It takes two months to go around the circuit once. Many of the churches are large, with several hundred people present every Sabbath. All told, there are fully 4,000 Christians in the churches under my care. The last time I went to Yung You, one of my country churches, seven hundred people met me for service Sabbath afternoon. The church was filled with women, the men sitting outside on mats under a canopy. I stood in a window, one leg inside and one leg outside the building, and preached the sermon. This growth is by no means peculiar to my own territory. Many of the missionaries have a much larger work under their care. In all Korea today there are not less than 250,000 Christians worshipping God in more than 2,000 places, where they have churches erected and supported almost entirely by themselves.

Several years ago an old widow named Kim-si, or daughter of Kim, heard how a certain woman once built a chamber for Elisha, putting in a bed and a seat and a candlestick. Kim-si thought that that would be a good thing to do for me, so when she built a new house she added a room for me, papering it with clean white paper decorated by a local artist, with pictures of birds and flowers. The idea spread to other churches until now, wherever I go, I generally find a room near the church freshly papered and prepared for me.

I am almost ashamed to tell how the Koreans love and honour their missionary pastor. Each of us has half a dozen or more Korean assistant pastors, or helpers, as they are technically called, who care for the churches during the missionaries' absence. Most of these men are students for the ministry and will some day be ordained and given full charge of churches as pastors. As yet, however, there are only a few ordained Korean pastors and the greater part of ecclesiastical authority is still in our hands.

Let me relate the actual happenings on my last country trip before leaving Korea on furlough. Dr Baird, Principal of our Pyengyang College and Academy, was absent last year on furlough, and Mr Bernheisel and I did the best we could to assist Mr McCune and keep the school running. It is no sinecure, I can tell you, to step from evangelistic work into a professor's chair in college and teach four or five hours daily such subjects as political economy, geometry and general history in the Korean language.

My country work necessarily had to be neglected. Some of the churches were visited only once last year. My last trip was made to Nam San Moru, a church of over two hundred Christians in a little valley twelve miles north of Pyengyang. I had been teaching in the college all the week and left for Nam San Moru on Friday afternoon after school on a little donkey, so small that my legs almost dragged on the ground, but surprisingly strong and pugnacious. My load had gone out on men's backs some hours before. Two men carried my boxes twelve miles for twenty-five cents apiece.

The road to Nam San Moru goes out through a gate north of our house in the old Ke-ja wall, three thousand years old. After a hard struggle with the donkey I finally got him saddled and we shot out through the gate and across the plain toward Nam San Moru, the donkey braying good-bye like a fog horn.

About two miles from Nam San Moru, I found a company of Christians waiting for me at a little village, with thirty school-boys drawn up in a straight line by the roadside. Nearly all the stronger churches have boys' schools and some have girls' schools. There are twenty-six church schools in the five counties under my care, all entirely supported by the Korean Christians.

After the greetings by the roadside were over, we started toward the village of Nam San Moru together, a small boy taking proud possession of my donkey, now quite tamed by the rapid ride, while I walked with the men. Just in front of the village we found the old woman and the girls from the girls' school, the latter dressed in rainbow-tinted dresses and drawn up in line, like the boys, to meet me.

The Nam San Moru church is a fine tile-roofed building, prettily situated in a cluster of oak trees behind the village. Here we assembled and each man came forward for his individual greeting. How they do love to be remembered! 'Nal amneka?' ('Do you know me?') is asked again and again; and how can I know them? Over four thousand Christians under my care and I able to visit them only twice a year! Why, I can scarcely keep track of the church officers, to say nothing of the hosts of new believers. One thing helps greatly. The Koreans are in tribes and most of them seem to belong to the Kim tribe. If I fail to recall a man's name, it is good policy to say, 'You are Mr Kim, aren't you?' and if I have been fortunate he will be delighted with my excellent memory.

Calling the officers, we went apart to a small room and prepared for business. First, the roll book was produced. Each church keeps an accurate record of the church attendance of all the Christians. A cross means 'present' and a cipher means 'absent'. Running my eye hastily down the list I found several names with only ciphers. Some proved to be sick or absent from the village, but several had fallen into sin and quit coming. 'Be sure and bring these men tonight,' I told the officers. 'Don't use force, but compel them to come if you can.'

We found twenty names on the roll of catechumens who had been attending faithfully for more than a year and were not yet baptized. The ordinary course is to receive a man publicly as a catechumen after he has been a Christian for three months and then one year later examine him for baptism. We sent for these twenty and examined them three at a time. Not a perfunctory, matter-of-course ceremony but a real examination, with a weighty decision at the close, whether baptism should be administered or not. 'How long have you been a Christian? Who is Jesus? Why do you believe in Him? Have you kept the Sabbath faithfully since believing? Can you read? Do you have family prayers in your home daily? Have you brought anyone to Christ?' We seek to discover through it all whether the person examined is sincere, looking earnestly for the fruits of the Spirit in the new life. If I find a man or woman under fifty who has not learned to read the Bible, or a man whose wife is not a Christian, I nearly always postpone the baptism till more convincing proof is given of real zeal and love for the Master. That night we voted to baptize seventeen out of the twenty.

While the examination was going on, the Korean boy who always travels with me had been busy getting supper ready in an adjoining room. As soon as opportunity offered, he served my meal on a little round table about a foot high. After supper we hurried to the church for service to find the building packed so that an aisle had to be cleared for me to reach the platform. It was then half-past nine o'clock. Most of the audience had been waiting since noon. The meeting was necessarily a long one. First came the singing and several prayers, then an election of deacons and a special offering for the helper's salary, which should have been taken before I came. After the reception of catechumens, I baptized the seventeen whose examinations had been satisfactory, and then several children. Next was the sermon, not a short one either, followed by public reproof and suspension of the three recreant members, and last of all the Lord's Supper, when a deep and solemn hush rested on the upturned faces and Jesus Himself drew near with His rich and unfailing blessing.

It was past midnight before the benediction came, and I was weary enough to sink to sleep where I stood; but no, the hardest task of all lay before me. The three men I had summoned were there. I had to take them apart and try to win them back to repentance. This is where the real test comes. This is where the Korean Church most needs us. They can win converts and preach the gospel better than we can. They can build their churches and support them; but they wait most of all for us to come and bring back those who have fallen away, who refuse their pleading. Only on one's knees, by prayer and entreaty and tears, can such work be done. Gratefully, I record the repentance of all three that evening.

THE BEST WAY TO UNDERSTAND THE WHOLE church is to know one congregation intimately. Let me introduce you to the church in Anju.

In the spring of my first year (1901–02) in Korea, Dr Moffett took me with him on a trip through his district north of Pyengyang City. After ten days of journeying from place to place, we came one evening to the walled city of Anju, the principal city between Pyengyang and Weiju on the Chinese border. The city proper is situated on the south slope of a range of low mountains guarding the Chung Chun river. The old Seoul–Pekin road, entering by the southeast gate, forms the main street of the city. Half-way up the mountain is a second, inner wall, and still farther up a third wall, the citadel, the last place of refuge in time of battle. The mountains are covered with old, gnarled and twisted pine trees. The city abounds in springs, several flowing from solid rock in steady crystal streams, ten inches deep and from four to six feet wide, all joining to form one broad brook and spreading into a lake inside the outer wall. The walls of solid masonry are formed of great stones, mostly cut, and built up to a height of twenty feet. Inside, the wall is banked with soil, thickly carpeted with grass and flowers and fringed with weeping-willow trees. Scores of little shrines are clustered along the wall among the willows, while back on the mountain side are several large temples. On the highest point is an altar where sacrifice is made to heaven.

The people of Anju are very proud of their blood and their ancient families. They are not so poor as many communities and consequently more conservative. Though Christian preachers, both foreign and native, had visited the city frequently, no visible impression had been made. We found only one man named Kim and his wife in the city, and a saloon-keeper's wife outside the city, who made any profession of Christ. Several Christians came in from surrounding villages and we met that night in the rear room of the saloon, Kim's house not being large enough to accommodate even the small company that assembled. Kim is a fine grey-bearded old gentleman with a hearty laugh and a violent temper. He used to preach to his neighbours about Jesus and if someone refused to believe or became abusive, old Kim would lose his temper and proceed to pound religion into him. I had to postpone his baptism two years till he learned to control his temper.

The next morning, Dr Moffett took me for a walk on the wall. Standing on a high point overlooking the city, he told me for the first time why he had brought me to Anju. 'This city,' said he, 'is one of the strategic places in north Korea, and I hope it may be assigned to you.' He showed me how the trade from the far-off Kang Kei region passed through Anju, and how a church planted here would do much to evangelize the entire area. I gladly consented to undertake the work if the Mission saw fit to appoint me to it. That fall (autumn) at Annual Meeting, the Anju work was assigned to my care. I put all my young enthusiasm into it, not forgetting Dr Moffett's counsel. Where I visited other cities once, I visited Anju twice, and God prospered the work from the beginning. In a short time a sufficient number of Christians had been gathered to buy a small straw-thatched house inside the city. Here we hung out our sign,

'Yasu Kyo' ('The Church of Jesus') and hoisted the national flag on Sunday to guide strangers to service.

In God's good providence, two splendid young men, just my own age, Christians from near-by villages, moved to Anju and engaged in business. They became the natural leaders. God prospered their business and they gave a tenth of their incomes to the church and much more than a tenth of their time, without other pay than the joy of service, to preaching the gospel and church work.

Matters stood thus in 1904, the year the Japanese–Russian War swept down upon us. Anju, like Pyengyang, became a Japanese centre even after the Russians had been driven far beyond the Yalu. During the first uncertain days of the war, we American missionaries were confined to Pyengyang by government order, and could do little but watch the Japanese troops march in and out of our city. Day by day they marched in from the south, storing their baggage on our college campus, and out the next morning by the Pekin road, right past our houses, silently, without martial music except the occasional call of a bugle. We heard from the Koreans that every Japanese soldier carried on his person some means of death in case of capture. They expected a desperate conflict and went forward by no means sure of victory, but determined to win or die. A great deal has been published concerning the hardships inflicted upon innocent Koreans by disorderly Japanese who followed the army. I can speak only in praise of the regular army. Although the troops had to be quartered throughout the city in Korean houses, not a single case of outrage was reported to us. Our rights as American citizens were scrupulously regarded.

Naturally, I was anxious about my country churches. As soon as it appeared at all feasible, I went to the Japanese

Resident in Pyengyang and asked permission to visit my country district. He consented and gave me a passport written in Japanese and English which proved of great service to me afterward. The English translation is odd, but interesting:

> 'Rev Wm. N. Blair. The above-named person,
> being American Reverend, is going in Anju,
> Sook Chun and Kai Chun for preaching, and
> will be allowed to pass freely without
> hindrance, and such assistance will be given
> as he may be in need of.
> Depot of Supplies in Pyengyang.
>
> To Japanese Depot of Supplies and Troops at
> the places in the bearer's trips.'

With this passport as security, I went freely among my churches, meeting troops everywhere, but receiving only courtesy and kindness. Later when the government railroad was finished, I found to my delight that the guards readily honoured my passport and let me ride on the construction trains without charge.

It was on this first country trip, during the Russo–Japanese war, that I came one evening in company with several Koreans to the main road in front of Anju and was surprised to find the telegraph wires cut south of the city. Reaching the city, we found the gates closed and Japanese soldiers on guard above them. We learned from Koreans living outside the wall that a company of four hundred Cossacks had suddenly come down from the north the day before, and after cutting the wires had taken up their position on a high hill to the east and opened fire on the city. There was only a small Japanese garrison in Anju at the time. Most of the Korean population fled in terror at the first shot.

Fortunately for the Japanese, they had discovered the Russians in time to telegraph the news before the wires were cut to Sook Chun, twenty miles south, where another small garrison of one hundred men was stationed. The Sook Chun company started out at once and ran the entire twenty miles to Anju without stopping.

Meanwhile a hot battle raged in Anju. All the extra guns the Japanese could spare were put in the hands of Koreans with the instruction, 'Never mind if you can't hit anything. Shoot and make a noise.' The Russians never knew the weakness of the place or they would have taken it at once by storming the walls.

When the Sook Chun company arrived, the Anju commandant threw open the gates and led out his men. Together the less than two hundred Japanese soldiers charged straight up the hill and drove the Russians pell-mell down the other side. Probably more Japanese were killed than Russians; but the point is that the Russians fled, leaving enough dead to make a large mound not far from the Kai Chun road east of the city.

This explained the shut gates. The Russians were still in the neighbourhood and the Japanese fearful of a second visit. Our problem was how to get into the city. Word had been forwarded to the Anju Christians to expect me that evening and it was time for service. Presently a Korean came, saying he could guide us over a breach in the wall. Very quietly we made our way along the wall, crawled on hands and knees up broken defiles half way between the gates, and were soon inside the city, being welcomed by our overjoyed brethren at the church. Not a single Christian had fled. Christianity is a religion of peace; but it is

amazing how it stiffens men's backbones and gives new
courage to defend their rights and homes.

We were busy that evening and all the next day at the
church. About four o'clock, several of us went for a walk.
I expected to be arrested and was not disappointed. The
first Japanese coolie who saw me started off on a run, and
in a few minutes a squad of soldiers came marching our
way on a double quick march and put us all under arrest.
I knew enough Japanese to say 'headquarters,' and to
'headquarters' we went, with a soldier on either side and a
crowd of excited coolies behind.

The commandant spoke a little English, though my passport would have been sufficient identification. With a flour-
ish, he dismissed the crowd, and escorting me into his
private apartment, entertained me with tea and cake and
the story of the battle the day before. He showed me a
heap of Russian fur coats and high boots, with guns and
swords discarded in the flight, and two Russian prisoners,
one a great bearded fellow and the other a mere lad. My
sympathies at the time were entirely with the Japanese;
but I shall never forget the feeling that surged over me as
I tried to talk to these two Russians. They were white men,
prisoners in the hands of an alien race, and all the blood
of our common heritage surged through my body in an
overwhelming wave of sympathy and desire to set them
free.

This battle gave us our new church in Anju. The Christians saw their opportunity. 'Everybody has run away,' they
said, 'and the soldiers are stabling their horses in the
houses. The bottom has dropped out of the price of
property. Now is the time to buy a new church.' It may
have been a bit canny; but what a splendid exhibition of
faith! One of the best houses in the city was offered for sale.

By strenuous efforts half the price was secured; but only half. Possibly, I might have advanced the balance needed; but it is against our Mission rules and policy to put American money in Korean churches. The temptation to do so is often great. They are so poor, how can they give all the funds necessary? Yet experience has proved that it is better to let them bear the burden alone and grow strong by bearing it. They always manage somehow. When every resource had seemingly been exhausted, Choi-si, a widow with some property but no ready money, came forward. 'We must have this house,' said she, 'and if you all agree, I will give my home in the country as payment and live in one room of the church as the keeper.' Choi-si's offer was accepted as a gift from God. In twenty-four hours the building was ours and Christian men were at work transforming it into a church.

In the fall of 1904, when the danger of Russian invasion had passed, we visited Anju again and it was during this visit that another important happening in the growth of the church occurred: the signal conversion of Chun-si, foster sister of Choi-si, who gave her home to help buy the new church building. These two women had been widows for many years, living together as sisters, highly respected in the community.

When Choi-si became a Christian and Chun-si refused to believe, it happened according to the words of the Master that a sword entered in. Chun-si not only refused to believe herself but opposed Choi-si having anything to do with 'the people of Jesus'. For thirty years the two had lived one life. Now Choi-si entered a new world of belief and friendship where Chun-si was left out. Loneliness and grief and bitter hatred of the Christians filled her heart. She became so violent a persecutor that possibly a desire to escape may have influenced Choi-si in her gift to the church, inasmuch as it was provided that she should occupy one of the rooms as keeper of the building.

If she sought to escape, she failed. Chun-si packed her goods and moved into the church with Choi-si. Here was a nice situation, an enemy in the camp, a heathen woman and a persecutor, so bitter that the sound of singing and of prayer drove her into a perfect frenzy. The Anju Christians seemed helpless. Nobody cared to carry the old woman into the street to scream and tear her hair and throw the city into an uproar. Their only hope lay in the strong hand of the missionary. I sent Chun-si word to quiet down or leave the church and for a time she behaved a little better; but when our women's Bible class began, the devil seemingly entered into her to break up the meeting. She abused all who came and cursed and swore so that the younger women were frightened away.

It was high time to act, regardless of consequences. I called Chun-si out and told her she must go. I was sorry; but she had behaved so outrageously that she would have to leave, and leave immediately. 'Very well,' she said, 'I'll go,' and in a perfect storm of anger, she rushed into the church, grabbed here and there for her belongings, bound them into a bundle, and tore out of the church, pouring out threats and imprecations upon all of us. That night we had peace. The next morning while the women were having prayers the door suddenly opened and Chun-si rushed in and threw herself on the floor in an attitude of prayer, exclaiming, 'Kedo-hapsata' ('Let's pray'). Everybody was nonplussed. Was the old woman pretending, or had contrition overtaken her at last? She had to repeat her request several times before anyone offered to pray.

Chun-si rose up from that prayer absolutely a changed

woman. In fact, the change came in the night, when, as she told us, alone and in a strange place Jesus came to her and opened her eyes. She sat through that class a repentant woman and an eager learner. What a miracle! She who once hated the very name of Jesus came overnight to love Him with a great love. The transformation of her face was beautiful to see. I had known her before to be a hard-visaged, hateful, blaspheming woman. Now all the hard lines were gone, driven out by the great peace and love that came to her self-tortured soul. Would that I could paint the two faces as they live in my memory! No better apologetic could be found for foreign missions.

The two sisters now went forth, hand in hand, to declare the gospel to their friends in Anju, and Chun-si soon became the greater power of the two. It was said of her, as of Saul of Tarsus, 'Is not this she who made havoc of them that called on this name?' Scores of men and women were converted. The Christians were no longer in confusion, but meeting together 'with gladness and singleness of heart, praising God and having favour with all the people. And the Lord added to them day by day those that were saved.'

In course of time, Chun-si became a catechumen, and after the usual year's instruction, was baptized, my hand sprinkling the baptismal water on the bowed grey head, and in my heart a profound sense of God's grace and presence.

Another year went by and once more Mrs Blair and I visited Anju together. The church was crowded for communion service on Sunday, but Chun-si was not there. She lay in a room not far away, listening to the singing, but unable to enter. After the service, Mrs Blair and I, with the officers and one or two old women, went to Chun-si's side and held a short service of song and prayer and I adminstered the communion. 'No,' she said, 'I am not afraid to die, but very tired and long to be with Jesus.' We never saw her again. Only a few days later God called her home with a song of praise on her dying lips, gloriously triumphant.

The winter before we left Korea on furlough, plans were begun for a new church in Anju, to be built on the hillside overlooking the city. Timber was purchased on a mountainside twenty miles away, cut down and hauled over the snow to Anju. When spring came, business halted while the foundation was being laid and the big timbers squared for raising. Much of the work had to be done by paid carpenters and masons; but all that unskilled hands could do was gladly done by Christians, for money is scarce in Korea. Saving everywhere possible, the church would cost fully 30,000 nyang, $1,500 in American money; but representing a sacrifice to them of $30,000. Nor was it easily raised, or all at one time. The congregation met time and time again to pledge the money. All gave what money they could, some gave their fields, others grain or merchandise; women gave their jewellery, and it was done.

Finally the frame was up, looming like a cathedral above the city, built to seat six-hundred and high enough to permit enlargement to seat twelve-hundred. I went to Anju on a visit of inspection and crawled all over the building with the building committee to see if the trusses were sufficiently strong, all of us happy as children. One thing troubled us. The contractor who had promised to furnish the tile went back on his bargain. The rainy season was drawing near and our building uncovered. Letter after letter reached me after I had returned to Pyengyang, telling of their anxiety, and asking me to ship tile from Pyengyang. I found this quite impossible. One day a letter came saying, 'Never mind, God has sent us the tile.' Where do you suppose the tile came from? I mentioned the spirit-shrines clustered under the willow trees on the wall surrounding the city. The magistrate of Anju sent word that if the Christians wanted tile badly, he would sell them all these shrines as they were no longer used by the people, and for a price he sold the church the whole collection, and the Christians went up in crowds and lifted the tiles from the roofs of the devil-houses, carrying them on their backs through the city, and setting them high on the house of God, greatly rejoicing; and all the city looked on, no one objecting!

8 : The Church's Testing

ENOUGH HAS BEEN GIVEN IN THE FOREGOING chapter to show the character of the Korean Church. There is no overstating the zeal of the Korean Christians, their enthusiasm in witnessing, their generosity in giving, their delight in prayer and the study of God's Word. It is a mistake, however, to suppose that there have been no difficulties to overcome, no problems, no times of testing. The Far East is in a ferment. The great wars that have shaken the nations and changed the course of history have focused in Korea during the short period of the Church's history. Nothing but the guiding presence of the Lord's Spirit has brought the Church in safety to this hour. Nothing but the Spirit of the Lord poured forth from heaven in Pentecostal power could have saved the Church at the time of its great testing.

The critical time to which we allude came with the establishment of the independent Korean Church in 1907. It has never been the thought or desire of the missionaries of our Church or of our Board of Foreign Missions that the churches established in foreign lands should be permanently under the direction and control of the American Church; but that just as soon as it seemed wise to take the step, independent churches should be established in the different countries, which should be encouraged to assume the full burden and responsibility of evangelizing their own lands.

Apart from the salaries and expenses of the American

missionaries and certain financial assistance given to our hospitals and a few high schools, the Korean church had been practically self-supporting for several years. We had ordained elders in many churches. Most of the direction of local affairs had already passed into Korean hands. Expecting also, as we did, that the Theological Seminary would graduate its first class into the ministry in 1907, the date of establishment of the Korean Presbyterian Church was set for that year. Including one elder from each organized church, the first Presbytery would have more Korean voting members than foreign missionaries, and the control and destiny of the Church would henceforth be absolutely in their hands. Of course, that was just what we wanted. We wanted a Korean church, not an American church. Nevertheless, we knew there was danger in thus entrusting power to untried hands. We were not ignorant of the experiences of our brethren in other lands. Nor were prophets of disaster wanting. Yet herein lies faith's victory. We had confidence in our Korean brethren. We knew that the marvellous development of the church was the work of God and not of man. So we made our plans for 1907. Announcements were out beyond the possibility of change or recall when the whirlwind of the Japanese–Russian War swept over the country and changed the face of everything.

Japan won and Korea went to the victor. It was easy for Japan because she already held the Korean peninsula. The Koreans had submitted without resistance to the military occupation of their peninsula by Japan, regarding it as a military necessity. Suddenly Korea awoke with a start. The war was over, and Japan, still in the peninsula, clearly had no intention of withdrawal. Hence Korea saw herself stripped of her dignity as an independent nation and humiliated beyond measure by the return of her foreign envoys, and the careless indifference, even contempt, of foreign nations.

In a day, that which centuries of misrule on the part of her own rulers had failed to do, the Japanese occupation accomplished: patriotism was born in Korea. A wave of intense national feeling swept over the land. 'Korea for the Koreans,' and, 'It is better to die than to be slaves' were sayings heard on every hand. Unable to resist the Japanese openly, secret meetings were held throughout the country. Many fled to the mountains, taking the name of 'we pyung,' or 'righteous army,' and waged guerrilla warfare on the Japanese. It is still dangerous for a Japanese citizen to travel alone far from the fortified cities.

Naturally there arose a call for every man to declare himself for or against the Japanese. All saw in the Church the only hope for their country. There is no denying the intense loyalty of the Korean Church. Christianity gives men backbones. There were not lacking many hotheads in the Church itself who thought the Church ought to enter the fight. The country wanted a leader and the Christian Church was the strongest, most influential single organization in Korea. Had she departed even a little from the strict principle of non-interference in politics, thousands would have welcomed her leadership and flocked to her banner. We might have again witnessed the cross of Constantine leading a great army. I believe Korea, like the Roman Empire, would have adopted Christianity in a day, and I believe, too, we would have had another Roman Church.

It took high courage, coupled with wisdom and great love to lead the Church aright, to stand up before men burning with indignation at their nation's loss and preach the doctrine of love and forbearance, and forgiveness even of enemies. Yet this is just what the missionaries and our best Korean leaders did. Thank God, the Church, as a whole, wonderfully taught of the Spirit, received our teachings as the word of God. But some were disobedient. Everywhere there was an element that turned its face away. Efforts were made to undermine the influence of the missionaries and church officers who advised submission. Some of the Korean leaders were openly called traitors, some had their lives threatened.

About this time, too, there returned to Korea a number of young men who had been in America long enough to get the 'big head.' Most of them professed to be Christians, but their Christianity consisted more of a desire to free their country, and of personal ambition, than of a sincere acceptance of Christ and a desire to do His will. These young men caused us much trouble. They told stories, all too true we were forced to admit, of the prevalence of immorality, of drunkenness and ungodliness in America. 'What right had these Americans, these foreigners, to lead the Church anyway!' Some went to the length of saying that the Americans even more than the Japanese were responsible for the unfortunate condition of Korea. At different times mobs arose and broke up our meetings. Those who were responsible for such disturbances were never numerous; but a few men can make a deal of noise. When men's hearts are wrung, a dozen wild-eyed agitators can do no end of damage.

The Koreans had long looked upon America as their special friend. Our ambassador, Dr Allen, enjoyed the confidence and esteem of the Korean King and of all the people. Great was the disappointment everywhere when the United States, following Britain's example, hastened to recognize Japan's control. A violent anti-foreign, especially anti-American, storm swept over the land. We bowed our heads, not to the storm, but to God in prayer. When men get terribly confused in their minds, when they get deadly hatred in their hearts towards those whom they regard as oppressors, when they grow cold toward their leaders and find the message of love and forgiveness unwelcome, then a condition of things is brought about that the devil knows well how to use. Men find it impossible to live up to the high standards of the Christian life in a heathen land without the Spirit's presence. Church members with hatred in their hearts simply lose God's help and fall easy victims to temptation. We were grieved again and again by the falling into sin of men we had trusted.

Have I made the situation plain? We were about to turn over the authority of our Church to Korean hands, to establish an independent Korean Church. Suddenly we found ourselves in the dangerous situation described. How could we take so critical a step at such a time? Yet we had to do what we had promised to do or break faith with our Korean brethren. So it was that God compelled us to look to Him.

IN AUGUST 1906, WE MISSIONARIES OF PYENGYANG, realizing the gravity of the situation, met together for one week of Bible study and prayer. Dr Hardy, of Won San, whom God has greatly blessed, came to Pyengyang to lead us. The First Epistle of John, which came to be our text-book during the revival, was selected for special study. How often God's Word seems written for special occasions! We were seeking help in time of need. The Apostle John assured us that everything depended upon fellowship with God, and that divine fellowship was conditioned upon love and righteousness. He who searches the deep things of the heart took the Epistle and made it a living, personal message. 'God is love and he that abideth in love abideth in God, and God in him.'

We had reached a place where we dared not go forward without God's presence. Very earnestly we poured out our hearts before Him, searching our hearts and seeking to meet the conditions. God heard us and gave us an earnest that week of what was to come. Before the meetings closed the Spirit showed us plainly that the way of victory for us would be a way of confession, of broken hearts and bitter tears.

We went out of those August meetings realizing as never before that nothing but the baptism of God's Spirit in mighty power could fit us and our Korean brethren for the trying days ahead. We felt that the Korean Church needed not only to repent of hating the Japanese, but a clearer vision of all sin against God, for many had come into the Church sincerely believing in Jesus as their Saviour and anxious to do God's will, without great sorrow for sin because of its familiarity. We felt that the whole Church, to become holy, needed a vision of God's holiness, that embittered souls needed to have their thoughts taken away from the national situation to their own personal relation with the Master. We agreed together at that time to pray for a great blessing upon our Korean brethren, especially at the time of the winter Bible-study classes for men in Pyengyang.

The Bible-study class system is a special feature of the Korean work. Each Church appoints a week or longer some time during the year for Bible study. All work is laid aside. Just as the Jews kept the Passover, the Korean Christians keep these days sacred to prayer and the study of God's Word. The result of such uninterrupted Bible study is inevitably a quickening of the entire Church, a true revival of love and service. Let America follow Korea's example in this one thing and the revival problem will take care of itself.

Besides the classes held in each church, and numerous county and circuit classes, each Station has one or more general classes where representatives from all the churches assemble in the centre where the missionaries live, and spend from ten days to two weeks in Bible study and conferences. The Pyengyang General Class for men is usually held during the first two weeks in January, the attendance averaging for years between eight hundred and a thousand. Most of these men walk to Pyengyang distances varying from ten to one hundred miles. All come at their own expense and pay a small tuition fee to defray the expenses of the class. The attendance from the country is so large that local Pyengyang Christians are barred from the Class to make room for the visitors, a special Class being held for Pyengyang merchants in February.

The General Class is divided into eight sections, each having, besides the morning devotional period and the half hour of singing, three full hours of Bible study under different missionaries and Korean teachers. At night a mass meeting for men is held at the Central Church, women being excluded for lack of room.

These Station Classes give invaluable opportunity to inspire and direct and unite the whole Church in its faith and life. The strongest men from all the churches are here. A new song taught in the Station Class will soon be sung all over the district. Every new thought and conviction sown here bears fruit in all the churches. This is why we prayed especially for the Pyengyang Bible Class.

The fall of 1906 was largely given up to country itineration. No special meetings could be held except during a few evenings in the Central Church at Pyengyang at the time of Dr Howard Agnew Johnson's visit immediately after the Annual Meeting in September. Dr Johnson told the Korean Christians about the blessings received in India and left a hunger in many hearts for similar manifestations of God's grace among us.

Christmas came and our scattered force assembled in Pyengyang to share the season's joys together. Usually we spend the week between Christmas and New Year's day getting acquainted with our families again, and resting in preparation for the busy days of the approaching Bible Class season. Frequently, the whole community will meet for a social evening, having the best time imaginable. That winter we had no heart for social gatherings. Prayer-meetings were held each evening. When the Presbyterian

Class began on the 2nd of January, the evening prayer-meetings had to be discontinued; but so strong was our desire to pray that we decided to hold noon prayer-meetings daily during the class for those who could attend. As Mr Lee says in his brief account of 'How the Spirit Came to Pyengyang, 'these noon prayer-meetings were a very Bethel to us.'

The evening meetings connected with the class began on the 6th of January in the Central Church with more than fifteen-hundred men present. Missionaries and Korean pastors led these meetings, all seeking to show the need of the Spirit's presence and the necessity of love and righteousness. The meetings were intensely interesting as meetings in times of crises always are. Nothing unusual happened. We were not looking for anything unusual. Only a hushed, solemn sea of upturned faces and eagerness to lead in prayer showed how the Spirit was working.

On Saturday night I preached on First Corinthians 12:27: 'Now ye are the body of Christ, and severally members thereof,' endeavouring to show that discord in the Church was like sickness in the body – 'and if one member suffers, all the members suffer with it' – striving to show how hate in a brother's heart injured not only the whole Church but brought pain to Christ, the Church's Head. Shortly after going to Korea, I had an accident while hunting and shot off the end of one of my fingers. All the Koreans knew of this. Holding out my hand, I told the congregation how my head ached and my whole body suffered with the injured finger. The idea seemed to go home to them. After the sermon many testified to a new realization of what sin was. A number with sorrow confessed lack of love for others, especially for the Japanese.

We went home that night confident that our prayers

were being answered. On the following Sunday night we had a strange experience. There was no life in the meeting. The church was crowded as usual, but something seemed to block everything. After the sermon a few formal prayers were offered and we went home weary as from a physical contest, conscious that the devil had been present, apparently victorious.

AT MONDAY NOON, WE MISSIONARIES MET AND CRIED out to God in earnest. We were bound in spirit and refused to let God go till He blessed us. That night it was very different. Each felt as he entered the church that the room was full of God's presence. Not only missionaries but Koreans testify to the same thing. I was present once in Wisconsin when the Spirit of God fell upon a company of lumbermen and every unbeliever in the room rose to ask for prayers. That night in Pyengyang, the same feeling came to me as I entered the room, a sense of God's nearness, impossible of description.

After a short sermon, Mr Lee took charge of the meeting and called for prayers. So many began praying that Mr Lee said, 'If you want to pray like that, all pray,' and the whole audience began to pray out loud, all together. The effect was indescribable – not confusion, but a vast harmony of sound and spirit, a mingling together of souls moved by an irresistible impulse of prayer. The prayer sounded to me like the falling of many waters, an ocean of prayer beating against God's throne. It was not many, but one, born of one Spirit, lifted to one Father above. Just as on the day of Pentecost, they were all together in one place, of one accord praying, 'and suddenly there came from heaven the sound as of the rushing of a mighty wind, and it filled all the house where they were sitting.' God is not always in the whirlwind, neither does He always speak in a still small voice. He came to us in Pyengyang that night with the sound of weeping. As the prayer continued, a spirit of heaviness and sorrow for sin came down upon the audience. Over on one side, someone began to weep, and in a moment the whole audience was weeping.

Mr Lee's account, written at the time of the revival, gives the history of that night better than any words, however carefully penned three years later, can do. 'Man after man would rise, confess his sins, break down and weep, and then throw himself to the floor and beat the floor with his fists in perfect agony of conviction. My own cook tried to make a confession, broke down in the midst of it, and cried to me across the room: "Pastor, tell me, is there any hope for me, can I be forgiven?" and then he threw himself to the floor and wept and wept, and almost screamed in agony. Sometimes after a confession, the whole audience would break out in audible prayer, and the effect of that audience of hundreds of men praying together in audible prayer was something indescribable. Again, after another confession, they would break out in uncontrollable weeping, and we would all weep, we could not help it. And so the meeting went on until two o'clock a.m., with confession and weeping and praying.'

Only a few of the missionaries were present on that Monday night. On Tuesday morning, Mr Lee and I went from house to house telling the good news to all who were absent, (and to our Methodist friends in the city). That noon the whole foreign community assembled to render thanks to God.

I wish to describe the Tuesday night meeting in my own language because a part of what happened concerned me personally. We were aware that bad feeling existed between several of our church officers, especially between a Mr Kang and Mr Kim. Mr Kang confessed his hatred for Mr

Kim on Monday night, but Mr Kim was silent. At our noon prayer-meeting on Tuesday, several of us agreed to pray for Mr Kim. I was especially interested because Mr Kang was my assistant in the North Pyengyang Church and Mr Kim an elder in the Central Church, and one of the officers in the Pyengyang Men's Association, of which I was chairman. As the meeting progressed, I could see Mr Kim sitting with the elders behind the pulpit with his head down. Bowing where I sat, I asked God to help him, and looking up saw him coming forward.

Holding to the pulpit, he made his confession. 'I have been guilty of fighting against God. An elder in the church, I have been guilty of hating not only Kang You-moon, but Pang Mok-sa.' Pang Mok-sa is my Korean name. I never had a greater surprise in my life. To think that this man, my associate in the Men's Association, had been hating me without my knowing it! It seems that I had said something to him one day in the hurry of managing a school field-day exercise which gave offence, and he had not been able to forgive me. Turning to me, he said, 'Can you forgive me, can you pray for me?' I stood up and began to pray, 'Apa-ge, Apa-ge' ('Father, Father,') and got no further. It seemed as if the roof was lifted from the building and the Spirit of God came down from heaven in a mighty avalanche of power upon us. I fell at Kim's side and wept and prayed as I had never prayed before. My last glimpse of the audience is photographed indelibly on my brain. Some threw themselves full length upon the floor, hundreds stood with arms outstretched toward heaven. Every man forgot every other. Each was face to face with God. I can hear yet that fearful sound of hundreds of men pleading with God for life, for mercy. The cry went out over the city till the heathen were in consternation.

As soon as we were able, we missionaries gathered at the platform and consulted, 'What shall we do? If we let them go on like this some will go crazy.' Yet we dared not interfere. We had prayed to God for an outpouring of His Spirit upon the people and it had come. Separating, we went down and tried to comfort the most distressed, pulling the agonized man to the floor and saying, 'Never mind, brother, if you have sinned God will forgive you. Wait, and an opportunity will be given to speak.'

Finally, Mr Lee started a hymn and quiet was restored during the singing. Then began a meeting the like of which I had never seen before, nor wish to see again unless in God's sight it is absolutely necessary. Every sin a human being can commit was publicly confessed that night. Pale and trembling with emotion, in agony of mind and body, guilty souls, standing in the white light of that judgment, saw themselves as God saw them. Their sins rose up in all their vileness, till shame and grief and self-loathing took complete possession; pride was driven out, the face of men forgotten. Looking up to heaven, to Jesus whom they had betrayed, they smote themselves and cried out with bitter wailing: 'Lord, Lord, cast us not away forever!' Everything else was forgotten, nothing else mattered. The scorn of men, the penalty of the law, even death itself seemed of small consequence if only God forgave. We may have our theories of the desirability or undesirability of public confession of sin. I have had mine; but I know now that when the Spirit of God falls upon guilty souls, there will be confession, and no power on earth can stop it.

THE PYENGYANG CLASS ENDED WITH THE MEETING of Tuesday night. The Christians returned to their homes in the country taking the Pentecostal fire with them. Everywhere the story was told the same Spirit flamed forth and spread till practically every church, not only in North Korea, but throughout the entire peninsula had received its share of the blessing. In Pyengyang, special meetings were held in the various churches for more than a month. Even the schools had to lay aside lessons for days while the children wept out their wrongdoings together.

Repentance was by no means confined to confession and tears. Peace waited upon reparation, wherever reparation was possible. We had our hearts torn again and again during those days by the return of little articles and money that had been stolen from us during the years. It hurt so to see them grieve. All through the city men were going from house to house, confessing to individuals they had injured, returning stolen property and money, not only to Christians but to heathen as well, till the whole city was stirred. A Chinese merchant was astonished to have a Christian walk in and pay him a large sum of money that he had obtained unjustly years before.

As soon as it was possible, I went to the country to look after my country churches. Everywhere I found the people already prepared, praying for the Spirit's blessing and not once did He disappoint us. Clearly it was the will of God that not one weak group nor one small child should miss the blessing. I remember two small boys, both nine years old, the only believers in their families, who came forward during the meeting at Yung You and wept grievously over their sins. After the meeting, they made me promise to pray daily for their unbelieving parents. Two years later I met the boys again. One brought his younger brother who had become a Christian with him and told me that his father had promised to become a Christian. The other stood just behind and said, 'My father is already a Christian,' the happiest boy imaginable.

One of my churches, Nam San Moru, was very weak and in a discouraged condition. The hour this church wept its sins out before God was an hour of new birth and power. Today, it is one of my strongest churches, with a congregation of three hundred. One afternoon during those long-to-be-remembered days, I found I could not keep an appointment to preach at So Kam, a goldmining camp where we had a few weak followers. Securing a horse, I rode to the church where the few Christians were assembled and told them that I must go back to the city at once, and that I would only wait to lead them in prayer. I had scarcely started to pray, when the same spirit of sorrow for sin fell upon that company of miners, some of them men who had lived hardened lives of sin before believing. I left them weeping together. That hour was also the beginning of new life and power for So Kam. They have recently built a fine new church that will seat over three hundred.

Some strenuous scenes were witnessed during the revival. At Yung You, where Mr Lee and I held a class for one week in February of that year, I saw a man arise and confess that he had killed a man in a valley not far from the church. So saying he fell unconscious before the pulpit so that we had to work over him to bring him to. Such sins cannot be confessed without the whole nature being torn as with a death struggle. It is remarkable, considering the intensity and wide extent of the revival, that no serious ill-effects were reported. The result was everywhere whole-some, except where men deliberately resisted or sought to deceive the Spirit and their brethren. At first we were greatly troubled lest, in the excitement, insincere confes-sions, perhaps from wrong motives, might be made; but we soon found that we could trust our people with God. Sometimes a man would get up and make only a partial confession of his wrongdoings, holding back the part he was really ashamed of; but the next night would find him back, pale and tortured, ready to rise at the first opportu-nity and confess his double sin in hiding his great sin the night before. Once the Spirit convicted a man, he seemed to get no rest day or night till he had unburdened his heart to the church and done what he could to repair the injury. Only in a few cases, where men guilty of sins which they refused to confess in spite of overwhelming conviction which made them writhe on their faces, was injury experi-enced. God waited long and seemed to put forth all his power to save such; but in the end, if they continued to re-fuse his pleadings, He turned from them and cast them out. Sooner or later the sin would be uncovered and the church learn just why it was that the brother had failed to find help and peace.

One of my helpers, the man named Kang, referred to as having been at enmity with Mr Kim, had a terrible experi-ence. Night after night he would be under conviction, never finding peace. After the revival was over, he gradually lost interest and we had to remove him from office. Finally he ceased coming and avoided me. A full year later, the con-fession of a woman proved this man Kang to have been guilty of immorality while he was a church officer. He refused to confess, resisting the Spirit to the end, and God let him go. Kang went from bad to worse, and finally became the keeper of a brothel in the city. Only a few months ago word reached me that he had attempted to end his life by taking opium.

Apart from a few cases like Kang's, the effect of the revival upon the Church was exceedingly helpful and uplifting. The whole Church was washed and made clean and sweet and new. When we met to organize our Independent Korean Church that fall (autumn), not a word was heard about fighting, only a great desire to pray and to preach the gospel as soon as possible to all Korea and, in God's will, to China and Japan. That first meeting of the new Korean Church was really a foreign missionary meeting. A Board of Foreign Missions was organized. The Presbytery laid its hands upon one of the first seven men to be ordained to the gospel ministry, the most gifted man in the class, Ne Ke-pung, and sent him as a foreign missionary to Quelpart, an island south of Korea. The missionary spirit has taken possession of the whole Church, especially of the young men in the College. Last year the Pyengyang College and Academy students raised enough money to send one of their own number, Kim Hyung-cha, to Quelpart, to help Ne Ke-pung. Kim Hyung-cha is one of our most promising young men. He would have graduated from college last year; but we had to hold up the graduating class for one year on account of insufficient teaching force. He was spending the year helping me in my office and teaching certain classes in the College. The committee met and elected Kim Hyung-cha to go to Quelpart without his knowledge. I was sent to see him about the matter and found him sick, lying on the floor at his home. I put my hand on his head. He was too feverish to talk so I simply said, 'Hyung-cha, the Missionary Committee met today and elected you to go to Quelpart; will you go? Don't tell me now: think it over and tell me tomorrow.' He told me later that he turned his face to the wall and fought the battle of his life. His salary as a missionary would only be a little over a half of what he was then receiving; besides, he was enjoying special opportunities connected with his work in the college, for music and language study. But the call conquered. The next day in answer to my question, he said, 'I will go.' He did go, and how the boys prayed for him all the year!

Last year another ordained man was sent by the Korean Church to Vladivostok in Russia, to preach to the thousands of Koreans who have settled in that area.

Part 2 : The Sufferings of
the Korean Church

by
Bruce Hunt

Dr Moffett's first house in Pyengyang. First church services were held here, and the first seven men were baptized here in 1894.

Central **Presbyterian** Church, Pyengyang. Built in 1900 to seat over 1500. Mother of 18 churches.

Part of the 1st United Presbytery of the Korean Presbyterian Church, September 17, 1907. This presbytery was the forerunner of the General Assembly which met in 1912. William Blair (author of the first half of this book) is in the back row, 7th from the left, between two Koreans. William B. Hunt (father of the author of the second half of the book), is seated in the front row at extreme left. The building behind is the Central Church where the revival started in Pyengyang.

A country church.

The First Seven Presbyterian Ministers. 1907.

One of the old gates to Pyengyang from the river. When Bruce Hunt was a boy he used to see the anchor chain of *The General Sherman* hanging from the corner of the roof of one of the other old gates to Pyengyang. It had been put there by the Koreans after the burning of the ship which carried Robert Thomas and the first Bibles brought to Korea.

Group of early missionaries. Left to right: William N. Blair, H. G. Underwood, Dr Sharrocks, William B. Hunt (father of the author) and Mr Welbon. With the exception of the third – a medical doctor – all were Presbyterian ministers.

The rugged and picturesque mountains of Korea have earned it the title of 'the Switzerland of Asia'. A suspension bridge in the Daedun mountains, 120 kilometres from Seoul.

The Blair home in Pyengyang

Dr Blair in the home of a Korean elder.

Dr and Mrs William N. Blair (right), the parents of Mrs Bruce Hunt, and the Rev. and Mrs Herbert E. Blair who worked for many years in Korea before moving to the Philippines. Herbert Blair died in a concentration camp in the Philippines in the Second World War.

Bruce Hunt alongside the Rev. Chun Bongsung (see page 126) with friends in South Korea shortly before the author returned to the United States in the summer of 1976. Bruce Hunt was born in Pyengyang where his father (William B. Hunt) first worked after arriving in Korea in 1897.

12 : The Background to the Sufferings during the Japanese Occupation, 1910–1945

KOREA WAS ANNEXED BY JAPAN ON AUGUST 22, 1910. Although the leaders of the Korean Church sought consistently to keep the Church free from political movements, and although the Holy Spirit cleansed and purified the Church in the great revival of 1907, many Japanese, especially police and military leaders, never understood the spiritual character of Christianity. Since their own national religion of Shinto was both religious and political, they were unable to rid themselves of the suspicion that the missionaries were political agents of their governments, and that the rapid growth of the Korean Church must be due to political reasons.

This was demonstrated in what became known as the 'Conspiracy Case.'

In October, 1912, three students of the Seoul Kyungsin Boys' High School (Presbyterian) were arrested. Later, all the teachers and many students were arrested. Further north, large numbers of people were arrested in Pyengyang, Syenchun and elsewhere, many of them leading Christians. The charge against them was not known at first. Shortly word began to leak out from the prisons of cruel tortures and beatings – the pouring of water down the nostrils of a man on his back, the driving of pieces of bamboo under the finger nails, the hanging up of people by their thumbs (tied behind their backs), the keeping of people in cramped cells where they could neither stand nor sit, or shocking them by first threatening them with red-hot irons, then applying ice-cold irons after the person had been blind-folded.

At about the same time a dramatic robbery had taken place in which a gang had made off with gold bullion being shipped from one of the American gold mines. The arrests were first rumoured as being in connection with this robbery. But then the government-controlled newspapers began to hint that a great conspiracy to kill the Japanese Governor General Terauchi, as he passed through Syenchun on December 29, 1910, had been uncovered and that this was the reason why 125 men (98 of them Christians) were to be indicted and brought to trial. This trial was held on the basis of the signed 'confessions' of the prisoners. Several missionaries (including Dr William N. Blair) were, according to the 'confessions', said to have had a part in the conspiracy. A Japanese Christian lawyer defended the prisoners. In the open court, all but one, who seemed to be mentally affected, professed innocence, declaring that the signed 'confessions' had been obtained under torture, and that there had been no conspiracy. In spite of the fact that the case could not be proved against them, 105 men were convicted. On appeal, however, all were acquitted except six men who were sentenced to ten years in prison, probably to save the face of the government. These men were all released after a few years. One of the six was Baron Yun Chiho, a prominent lay leader of the Methodist church and uncle of the second President of the Republic of Korea.

In Dr Blair's opinion, notwithstanding the hardships brought to many Christians, the 'Conspiracy Case' proved of real service to the Church. It cleared the atmosphere and removed much of the government's suspicion of missionaries and the Church. After the case relations with the government improved markedly.

The next period of suffering came in 1919. Korea had been under Japan for only nine years when Woodrow Wilson, at the close of World War I, presented his famous 'fourteen points' to the League of Nations. Among them was 'the self-determination of small nations'. The Korean leaders felt that silence at such a time would indicate their satisfaction with being ruled by Japan. A Declaration of Independence was secretly drawn up and signed by thirty-three prominent leaders in Korea. Fifteen of the signers, including the Rev Kil Sunjoo, a nationally beloved evangelist and Bible teacher, were Christians. This declaration was secretly distributed at predetermined times and places throughout the country, and publicly read amidst cheers of 'Tai Han Tong Nip Mansei' ('10,000 years to the independence of Korea'). The Christians had joined on the condition that violence should not be used. This condition was written into the Declaration itself.

The Japanese authorities, taken wholly by surprise, retaliated ruthlessly. The writer saw crowds of people, who would not even arm themselves with sticks or stones, charged with bayonets, and heard rifles fired at demonstrators. Mission hospitals were filled with wounded. Many were killed, others were beaten and mangled, still others suffered from the terrible conditions in the overcrowded prisons. The writer remembers the long lines of wounded prisoners, which the children stopped their play to watch, as they were brought in, almost daily, during March and April 1919, from the surrounding country areas where demonstrations were still going on.

The place of leadership which Christians had in many communities, their lively interest in social questions, and the fact that, in a country where less than five per cent of the people were Christians, fifteen out of the thirty-three signers were Christians, caused the Christians to be singled out more than others and a disproportionate number of Christians suffered. In Suwon, the whole congregation was called to the church, the building set on fire, and those attempting to escape shot down. Many Koreans, but especially Christians, fled to Manchuria and Siberia. The effects of that dispersion were still being felt half-a-century later. Those who were imprisoned preached to their fellows, leading many to Christ. Others in solitary confinement studied and memorized long passages of the Bible which they used later with telling effect in their ministries.

The brutality with which the authorities put down this movement aroused the sympathy of the civilized world when the news finally leaked out, and the Japanese government, in the face of world public opinion, replaced the militaristic government with a more moderate government, under Baron Makoto Saito, a liberal-minded man, friendly to Christianity, as Governor General. But the Church did not have peace for long.

From the time of the Japanese annexation of Korea one chief cause of tension between the government and the Church was over the matter of education. A law on education, enacted in 1911, stated the objective of education as the making of 'loyal, good subjects'. All schools were to be registered with the government within ten years, and no school could be registered except on the government's conditions. Among others, the conditions demanded that the government's curricula must be followed, most of the teaching was to be done in Japanese, teachers had to be approved by the government and could not be dismissed without the permission of the government, and finally, religious services could not be held or religious instruction given in these schools.

The missionaries of the Northern and Southern Presbyterian Missions were especially strong in their opposition to having mission schools registered under these conditions. In particular, the forbidding of religious instruction prevented the schools from being Christian schools in the true sense of the word. Some missions argued that education, as such, is a good thing, whether imparted by Christian teachers or not, and, if sponsored by Christians, could be called Christian education. Others argued that any education, as long as it was carried on by Christian teachers, even if formal Christian teaching was not allowed, was Christian education; and did not such education given by Christian teachers serve as a kind of bait, drawing people to Christianity, and giving teachers an opportunity to influence pupils outside school hours? But others held that that only can be designated Christian education in which Christian teachers teach the various subjects and are free to give Christian instruction beside and together with those subjects.

After the 1919 'Independence Movement', under the liberal Governor General, Baron Saito, the regulations were changed to allow for two kinds of schools – 'registered' and 'designated'. 'Registered' schools were those which fully met the government standards, including the exclusion of religious instruction from the curriculum. 'Designated' schools had to meet all the other government requirements, but were allowed to give Christian instruction.

But problems still remained. Qualified Christian teachers willing to accept positions in Mission schools, were often turned down by the government. Mission school Principals combed the Japanese empire for Christian teachers, who would also be acceptable to the Japanese authorities.

Furthermore, good Christian students were often reluctant to enrol in a 'Designated' school because those holding diplomas from 'Designated' schools were always considered to have a second-rate education, no matter how high the school's standards of education might be, and met with difficulty in transferring to, or getting into, 'Registered' High Schools and Universities for further studies. Difficulty was also encountered in getting the usually better-salaried government jobs after graduation.

Moreover, in the contracts under which the schools were designated, the Japanese authorities kept one condition that was later to be used tellingly against the Mission schools. It was that the objective of education was the making of 'loyal, good subjects'. In accepting this condition, the Mission authorities reasoned that there is nothing that will make a person a 'loyal, good subject' as much as leading him to be a good Christian. When the military clique began to make itself felt in the Japanese government, however, its interpretation of this was that 'loyal, good subjects' were those only who showed reverence to the Japanese Emperor, (who was considered a deity) by bowing before shrines, to the east, or towards the Emperor's palace – in other words, by participation in Shinto ceremonies. The word Shinto means 'the way of the god' or 'the way of the gods'. The ceremonies are usually conducted at a 'Jinja' which means a 'spirit house'. Shinto priests often officiated even at 'patriotic Shinto' ceremonies, calling spirits, and addressing words of comfort or prayers of adoration or thanksgiving and petition to them.

At first, there was little question in anybody's mind about the religious and non-Christian nature of the ceremonies. As the Korean pastors of one Presbytery put it, 'We know that the worship of deified spirits at the shrines is contrary to God's command'. At the time that the issue was being sharply debated, a Japanese official himself said, 'The great majority of the Japanese people believe that spirits are being worshipped in these (patriotic Shinto) ceremonies'.

But Christians, often faced with the alternative of losing their jobs in the school or government, or with expulsion from school, or with the closing of institutions built up through years of sacrifice, sometimes felt able to rationalize themselves into accepting the government's distinctions between 'religious Shinto' and 'patriotic' or 'State Shinto', and attending ceremonies at Shinto Shrines as a 'patriotic act'. An attempt to draw parallels between such ceremonies and the laying of wreaths on the tomb of 'the unknown soldier' in the west, or saluting the flag, was often made.

A majority of the Northern Presbyterian missionaries and the Southern Presbyterian missionaries, the latter with the firm backing of their home Board, took a strong stand against shrine worship, and closed mission schools in the Southern Presbyterian area immediately, rather than have the pupils or teachers participate in shrine ceremonies as representatives of the mission schools. The majority of the Northern Presbyterian Mission opposed shrine worship but was handicapped in making as clear a testimony by a vigorous minority, backed by the home Board, which did not take such a serious view of shrine worship. Eventually however, the Northern Presbyterian Mission closed its schools or, under pressure from the Board, turned some over to Koreans (a compromise move) to operate.

In the meantime, there were individual cases of teachers who were imprisoned or deprived of their teaching certificates, and of students who were expelled from school or even imprisoned. In 1935, the lives of Dr George McCune and (later) of Dr Samuel A. Moffett, who were in charge of Soongsil College, and Soongsil Academy in Pyengyang, were threatened by members of a fanatically nationalistic organization of Japanese ex-soldiers. Police 'protection' seemed designed more to hamper movement, and the police were not able to give any assurance of the safety of the missionaries' persons. Dr McCune and Dr Moffett, who had spent long years of fruitful service in the establishing of the Korean church, were forced to leave the country almost secretly, as though they were common fugitives from law.

Originally it had been represented that shrine worship was necessary only for students to make them 'loyal and good subjects'. But, after Japan invaded Manchuria in 1931, and launched out on her 'holy war' against China (1937), the military clique, who were now in the driver's seat, insisted that loyalty must be shown through shrine worship by all subjects. School children were made to put up shrines in their homes, as well as to bow to the one in the school yard every day and at the larger public shrines on special occasions. People working in public offices were made to bow to shrines in the offices daily and at public shrines on special occasions. Later it was insisted that all public meetings, including such diverse Christian services as Presbytery and General Assembly meetings, and Women's Missionary Society meetings, be opened with some form of patriotic Shinto bowing. Eventually, it came down to compulsory village, then house by house, representation and sometimes even to 'every individual' attendance at Shinto ceremonies.

The penalties for non-attendance or opposition to Shinto

ceremonies were of varying degrees. In a police state, where almost everything one does depends on permits, there were countless ways in which public officials could slow down, and make almost ineffective, anything attempted by one who was in their 'black books' for failing to co-operate in Shinto ceremonies. In the war years of rationing, one's stomach was touched and life itself threatened by the mere refusal of a ration card to a 'non-co-operator'. Children were beaten or expelled from school and even imprisoned for refusing to bow at shrines.

Informers kept the police posted on the teaching of missionaries, ministers and even of ordinary laymen. Some people, and the writer was one of them, had to notify the police of their movements about the country, reporting at the local police station whenever they arrived or left a town.

In Manchuria, the Rev Lloyd Henderson, a Presbyterian missionary working among Koreans, was shot and killed while travelling on a moonlight night under Japanese military guard. It was alleged that his death was the result of the party being fired on by bandits but the circumstances made a different explanation very probable. In Chungju, the Rev Otto De Camp and Dr D. S. Lowe of the Northern Presbyterian Mission were imprisoned for removing a small unwanted Japanese shrine from the home of one of the Korean workers living on mission property. They were in the penitentiary for several months and treated like ordinary criminals, being made to walk to trial bare-footed, with hands bound and a basket-like hood over their heads to prevent them from being recognized by passers-by.

Slapping and kicking were almost the routine treatment for Koreans being interrogated by the police. Prison diet was intended barely to sustain life. Many were tortured and beaten into insensibility. Heatless cells caused much suffering. Lice, fleas, and bedbugs were the prisoners' constant companions. The odour of the 'toilet' kept in the cell, and only emptied occasionally; the lack of liberty to get medical attention when needed; the absence of reading and writing materials, and the gaolers' sadistic delight in making life miserable for prisoners – all combined to cause one to prefer a quick martyr's death to the prolonged living death, no less a martyr's, which was the daily experience of those who survived.

The threat hung over the whole church. Several had already been in prison once or twice over opposition to shrine worship, when the matter was finally forced by the Japanese government on the General Assembly of the Korean Presbyterian Church for decision in 1938.

By orders from the top, commissioners to the Assembly were first dealt with individually in their home areas, where they were known and where the authorities had many ways of making life difficult for non-co-operators. They were given the choice of: (1) going to the Assembly and voting that shrine worship was not sinful; (2) going to the Assembly, but keeping silent on the shrine issue; (3) not going to the Assembly. The Rev Kim Sundoo refused all three, and attempted to go to the Assembly anyway, to make his protest, but was arrested and taken off the train and held in prison until the Assembly was over.

The missionaries, too, had been individually, and then collectively, warned that they were not to say anything on the subject, as it was a matter for the Koreans to settle. They had been ordered not to discuss the matter.

To these measures the authorities added the precaution of having plain-clothes men follow each commissioner to the Assembly from his home town, so that the fateful

Assembly was held in the atmosphere of an armed camp. Armed police, dressed as for a riot, guarded all entrances. None but commissioners, with their plain-clothes men shadows, were allowed in the West Gate Church in Pyeng-yang where the meeting was held.

All commissioners were ordered to go as a group to worship at the shrine before the opening of Assembly. The convening of Assembly was delayed for the arrival of high police authorities who were given places of honour at the front of, and facing, the Assembly.

When the actual motion, declaring shrine worship per-missible, was proposed, the moderator, acting under orders from the government, refused to allow any speeches except those favouring the motion. Dr Blair, followed by the Revs Kinsler and Hill, sought the floor and when it was refused, lodged their protests. The writer also seeking the floor to make a point of order, and demanding his right as a commissioner to speak, was physically forced from the floor by the police stationed around the auditorium, and only released on orders from their chief.

The motion was put, and received a weak affirmative vote. The negative was not put, but the moderator declared the motion carried. Again protests were not allowed. A committee of missionaries drew up a written protest which was signed by all the missionary commissioners, but the police prevented it from being recorded in the Assembly minutes, despite the common rule for the treatment of protests.

Another matter which came up at the same muzzled Assembly was the approval of a long disputed law on con-trolling religious activities. The government had enacted a law in which places of religious worship, and the right to conduct any form of religious worship or teaching, were made dependent on government permit. The question was whether the Assembly would approve conforming to this law. Should man ask permission of the government to do what God had commanded? As the Rev Lee Moonju of Taegu, whose saintly leadership and stand were clearly known, noncommittally put it at the time, 'We may today pass a motion agreeing to conform to this law, but in doing so we will go contrary to what Presbyterians have always stood for.'

Up to the time of the General Assembly's compromising action, individuals who were being pressured to worship at shrines could claim the backing of the greater numbers represented by the church and its laws. Furthermore, as the Japanese constitution guaranteed religious freedom, they felt comparatively safe when they could appeal to the law of the church. Now, any who refused to worship at the shrines could be represented by the government as individual fanatics, not even recognizing the laws of their own church, and probably with some motive of rebellion against the government behind their actions. Every man now had to stand on his own feet. The Korean church had come into the 'Valley of Decision'.

Church leaders were the special targets. Some went to Japan 'for post-graduate studies' to hide under the anonymity of a student's role. Others secreted themselves in country places until their identity was discovered and they could hide themselves no longer, then they fled elsewhere. Some left the ministry and went into secular work. Still others went to Manchuria or China where it was mistakenly thought that the government was so busy waging the 'Holy War' against China that it would not have time to search out non-conformists in the church.

Many broke under the strain. There was the evangelist

who worked with me. He had known prison before, during rioting in his student days. 'I could die for Christ,' he said, 'but I cannot endure the thought of years in prison, just deteriorating mentally and physically.' And one of the Korean ministers told me, 'It is different for you Americans; you can go to your homeland and get away from it; but for us Koreans there is no place to which we can escape.' When I suggested that death for Christ was a way of escape, he said, 'But I do not want to die.'

One case was that of the minister whose health had already been badly affected during a past imprisonment. He said that, for himself, he was willing to die, but what would become of the lambs and weak ones in the flock, the ignorant old women, the illiterate poor, and the children? If he refused to compromise, the church doors would be closed, he would be imprisoned, and they would have no place to go to in which they could hear the words of life. Others worried about who would care for aged parents, wives and children.

Laymen with convictions were also soon brought to light, as the government began to demand shrine worship in local churches, then on the home and even individual level. Now, they too began to be hounded like the leaders.

While some broke, others stood firm. There was the poor pop-corn vendor, known to the writer, in Manchuria, who did not yield even when deprived of his livelihood by the cutting off of his corn and kerosene ration because he would not contribute to the building of a local shrine.

There was the mother, arrested, (while heavy with child) because she had taught her daughter, the head of her class in school, to be willing to forfeit her education rather than bow at the shrine. The Japanese Principal of the school, though believing that he had to expel the girl for the sake of school discipline, wept as he did so at losing one of his better pupils.

There was the deaconess, and her husband, who, with a one-month-old baby on her back, was imprisoned because, with other members of the congregation, she had declared herself against shrine worship.

There was the fifteen-year-old son of Evangelist Lee Yonghee (one of the martyrs) who was locked up for standing with his father against shrine worship.

There was the bearded farmer, Chun Choisun, a 'Yung-soo' or church leader, and his grown son, Deacon Chun Choonduk, who were sentenced to six and eight years respectively, and only released by the ending of World War II.

Or again there was the godly nurse, Miss Kim Taekyung, working with Doctor and Mrs Roy Byram in their mission dispensary in Harbin, who was arrested, and sentenced to eight years in prison for opposing Emperor worship.

These are just a few of the cases known personally to the writer, but their stories were matched all over Korea. The same thing went on from Koje and Namhae Islands off the south coast of Korea to the Siberian border in Manchuria.

The years that have passed since Korea obtained her independence from Japan have convinced me of one thing: no one person knows or ever will know the number and names of all of those who died as a result of their testimony against shrine worship. At one time I was able to collect a list of over thirty who unmistakably died for their faith over the shrine issue. Dr Allen Clark says 'more than fifty church workers suffered martyrdom.'* Space and time do

* *History of the Korean Church*, A. D. Clark, 1961, p. 202. There were also those who suffered as much as, or more than, some of those who died.

not permit chronicling the stories of all of those that we know about. Having tried above to give a picture of the over-all struggle which produced the martyrs of this period, I will give in the next chapters a few of the cases of the witnesses who endured persecution unto death.

13 : Five of the Faithful unto Death

THERE WERE FOUR GENERAL AREAS IN WHICH THE Korean opposition to shrine worship seemed more especially concentrated, and even somewhat organized: South Kyungsang Province, the city of Pyengyang, North Pyengyang Province, and Manchuria. No area, however, was without its individual and in some cases corporate witness. The ringing witness of the Southern Presbyterian missionaries in the Chulla provinces, in closing the mission schools rather than compromise, has already been mentioned.

In South Kyungsang Province a team composed of the Revs Han, Choo, and Choi, and Evangelist Whang, toured the churches, strengthening the faith of the Christians. Several of the martyrs, and nine of those held by the Japanese in the Pyengyang penitentiary to the end of the war, were from this province.

In Pyengyang, the strong fight put up by the missionaries, together with the Christian institutions and churches, and especially a regular day-break prayer-meeting in the home of Rev Dwight Malsbary of the Independent Board, attended by many Koreans, seemed to have effects reaching all parts of Korea.

In North Pyengyang Province the movement seems to have centred around several dynamic individuals who moved among the people. The comparatively longer sentences which were to be given by the Japanese court to Rev Lee Kisun and to Evangelist Kim Ninhee bear out what I have heard of the activities of these two men in

North Korea in strengthening God's people and helping them to stand.

In Manchuria, a covenant binding a number of the Christians together in nonconformity to the shrine worship, proved a source of strength and it warrants some explanation at this point.

After the Presbyterian General Assembly had compromised on the Shrine issue in 1938, some Christians withdrew from the compromised church and began meeting separately for worship, some of them fleeing to Manchuria. The problem arose as to who should be invited to lead such meetings. Could Christians who had not formally broken from the compromised church, but who might attend such meetings, be asked to lead? Several of those, men and women, who were later imprisoned, including Kim Yoonsup, Bible Woman Kim Sinbok, and Bible Woman Pak Myungsoon, met in our home for a couple of days, after a full day of fasting and prayer, to discuss the matter.

Following the example of the Scottish Covenanters, a statement was drawn up, pointing out the Biblical teaching on shrine worship and the necessity of breaking completely from those who condoned idolatry. From then on, no one was baptized who did not give consent to this document, and no one was allowed to lead services who had not subscribed to it. There were about 25 small Korean Christian groups in north Manchuria which subscribed to this covenant, with just a little short of 500 covenanted baptized members and an average attendance for all the groups of about 800 people on each Lord's Day.

This covenant, drawn up in Harbin, north Manchuria, was later used by other groups throughout Manchuria and Korea, and I found it in use in Pusan, at the southern tip of Korea, in 1946, when I returned to Korea at the end of World War II.

PASTOR CHOO KICHUL

The most widely-known martyr of this period was the Rev Choo Kichul, Pastor of the Sanchunghyun Presbyterian Church in Pyengyang. Pastor Choo was born in 1897 in the town of Oongchun, South Kyungsang Province. He was the fourth son of a non-Christian family. Though his father was not a Christian, he seems not to have seriously opposed Christianity.

After grammar school, Choo went to a well-known Christian private school in North Korea, known as Ohsan Academy. This was not a mission school, but one started by Korean Christians. The Principal was a man of strong Christian character, having a moulding effect on the lives of the young people who studied under him. He was also a real Korean patriot. His love of his country and people carried over to his students. Choo became a nominal Christian during his five years at Ohsan Academy. Dr Arch Campbell, in *The Christ of the Korean Heart* says that it was under the preaching of Kim Ikdoo, that Choo came to experience what it was to be born again.* He attended Chosen Christian College (now Yonsei University) and Pyengyang Presbyterian Theological Seminary. Following his graduation from Seminary, he served churches in Pusan and Masan, in south Korea, before being called to the large Sanchunghyun Presbyterian Church in Pyengyang. Though still comparatively young, he was recognized as a leader in the Korean Presbyterian Church, and was one of the wiser heads seeking to hold the Church together

* *The Christ of the Korean Heart*, 1954, p. 57.

when the denomination was torn by sectional factions. He was a man of keen intelligence and good education, with dignity and restraint in speech and action. I especially recall his address at one of the General Assembly's day-break prayer meetings, shortly before his arrest. Though he did not mention the shrine issue specifically, his quiet, forceful, unfolding of God's Word left no doubt in the minds of his hearers what he believed the stand of the church should be in the matter of shrine worship. It was a refreshing breath of clear talk in a time of much confused thinking.

Though Choo's stand was common knowledge, at first the authorities hesitated to imprison him for his opposition to shrine worship, because the Japanese Constitution guaranteed 'freedom of religion'. A deacon in Choo's church, however, was a member of the 'Christian Farmer's Movement' which was under suspicion of the police as being a front for anti-Japanese, patriotic activities, and Choo was first arrested in 1938, as being, through the deacon, connected with this movement. He was taken to a prison in Weesung and held for half a year. He spent much of his time praying, reading, and memorizing the Scriptures. While the supposed cause for his arrest was his political activities, his opposition to shrine worship did not go unnoticed, and was brought up in the trial, in Taegu. He was acquitted of the political charge but threatened before being released.

On his first Sunday after release, he spoke for an hour, repeating Scripture verses in regard to tribulation, which he had memorized. As usual detectives were in the audience. Later, after much prayer, he preached with great freedom on the subject of shrine worship, declaring that bowing at shrines was idolatry. This was in August, 1939. He was arrested again. It was not easy to go. His blind mother, eighty years old, asked 'Where are you going?' and 'Why are you leaving me?' His children were crying. But as in so many of the cases of those who were enabled to be faithful to the end, he was backed by a consecrated wife, a real 'prayer warrior'. She would not pray for her husband's release, but that the Lord would help him to 'Be strong and of good courage to the end, and to be offered up a sacrifice on the altar of the Korean Church.' His congregation, too, backed him with their prayers, not for his release but that he would be 'faithful to the end'.

The authorities brought pressure on the Presbytery to declare Choo's pulpit vacant, after his arrest, and to replace him with a compromising minister. The congregation refused to listen to the traitorous Committee from Presbytery, singing 'A Mighty Fortress is our God' over and over for several hours to drown the voices of the Committee members. Police attempted to break up the meeting, roughly handling men and women alike, including white-haired Mrs Bernheisel, a senior missionary, who had been helping with the women's work of the congregation for many years. The congregation met every morning at 5 a.m. to pray for their pastor, even in the cold and dark of the winter months.

On the occasion of his second arrest his examination was accompanied by flogging from 9 a.m. to 2 p.m. and he finally fainted. Altogether he was examined under torture ten different times, but did not give in. Kim Yangsun was in the same cell with him, and they would often have prayer together. Kim Yangsun, who was later released, reports that he would often pray, 'Lord, don't leave this weak Choo Kichul too long, but hurry up and take him away'.

Choo was in prison for six years. During his last twenty days he was able to eat practically nothing and his body wasted away. His wife, though herself ill, visited him in prison on what turned out to be the next to his last day on earth. He was aware that death was near, and thought about where his body should be laid. When the prison guard suggested that Mrs Choo take her husband home to die, Choo said, 'Where will I go? This is my house'. And to his wife he said, 'Leave two more places on Tol Pak Mountain', referring to burial places, probably for his mother and his wife.

That his twenty days of not being able to eat was not a self-inflicted fast can be seen in the words showing that he longed to have a change from the rough prison diet for his disease-ridden body, 'I wish I could eat some Meem' (a mild Korean gruel).

Mostly there was concern for the church: 'I'm going, but what of the Sanchunghyun sheep?' 'I'm going to the Lord and will pray for the Sanchunghyun Church and for the Korean Church for ever, so be at peace.'

There was a close understanding between husband and wife, often mistakenly thought by occidentals not to exist among orientals: 'I've gone the road I'm supposed to go' – 'Follow in my steps' – 'Let's meet in heaven.'

Pastor Choo died at 9 : 30 p.m. on April 13, 1944.

That his light, which shone so far, also shone brightly at home is witnessed not only by the closeness of understanding between husband and wife but also in his children. One, especially, was outstanding, an evangelist in North Korea. I never met him, but the crop of keen, consecrated, young men, able in God's Word, now serving in churches throughout South Korea, who came from this young evangelist's church during the time of his ministry, is exceptional. It has made me often wish that I could have met this young man who so powerfully moulded many lives for good. He

K.P.—7

was later martyred under the Communists and has gone to join his father in the great 'cloud of witnesses', that 'multitude which no man could number' who stand 'before the throne and before the Lamb.'

ELDER PAK KWANJOON

Elder Pak Kwanjoon was rather widely known throughout the nation because he, with his son and Miss Ahn Eesook, a public school teacher, carried the protest against shrine worship into the almost 'sacred halls' of the Imperial Diet in Japan.

Elder Pak was born on the 13th of April, 1875, in Yengbyen, in North Pyengan Province. He came from a well-to-do family and in his boyhood studied the Confucian classics and Buddhism.

He became a Christian in 1905 and in 1910 undertook the study of medicine, starting a small hospital in 1914. He became more and more interested in preaching the gospel, and in 1921 left his hospital work to give full time to preaching as a layman. In 1923 he started a church in the Anju district in South Pyengan Province. As the years went by, the burden of speaking out against compromise with Shintoism became heavier upon him. In 1937, he decided to speak out publicly to Governor General Minami. He also wrote letters to prominent public officials and leaders in the church in Japan. This called the attention of the police to him, and he began to be followed by detectives.

Though Elder Pak did not have a great deal of money, he decided he must go to Japan and make his protest to the Diet itself. People thought he was foolish. Travel within the country was constantly being checked by the police and he was already a marked man. However, he felt the compulsion of the Lord's will upon him and started out. He asked the police for a travel permit to Japan, but was refused. One night he seemed actually to hear a voice saying 'Go to Japan', so, permit or no permit, he started out with his son and Miss Ahn, the public school teacher, who also felt the necessity of making this testimony. Strangely enough, they had no difficulty on the train or even on the ferry-boat across to Japan. People just thought he was an old Japanese man returning to his home country with his son and daughter.

In Japan, they first visited certain prominent Christian leaders and narrated the plight of the Christians in Korea. They also had the names of certain prominent Japanese statesmen who were known not to be sympathetic with the military clique. They were believed to hold that the military clique were making a serious political mistake in estranging the Korean people through their insistence on shrine worship. Through one of these statesmen, they were able to secure visitor's passes to the Diet building, something not easy to come by in those days of rising war tensions and suspicions in the Japanese Empire.

They made one visit to the Diet building just to get the lie of the land, then on March 21, 1939, they entered the building with leaflets hidden in their clothing. Again, providentially, the leaflets were not discovered when their persons were searched as they entered the building. What they were contemplating was looked on as an act of suicidal recklessness for colonial Koreans. In this same period ruling Japanese military fanatics had resorted even to the assassination of popular Premier Saito, to remove any obstacle to their programme of world conquest.

The 400 members were gathered for the 74th meeting of the Japanese Diet. At the time the Diet was especially considering the Religious Law. At first the three took their places in the gallery, Miss Ahn on the women's side. At a given signal, Elder Pak cried, 'It is the great purpose of Jehovah God', and with these words they threw the leaflets which they had prepared among the members of the Diet.

Elder Pak's leaflet urged the Japanese government to cease from its rebellion against God in forcing shrine worship on its people, lest the wrath of God fall upon the country. Pak's leaflet (1) urged that Christianity be made the national religion of Japan, and (2) warned that if Japan continued to persecute Christianity, she would be destroyed.

The scattering of the leaflets, of course, caused quite a commotion. The three were imprisoned for a month, then sent back to Korea. It resulted in the Diet appointing a Committee to investigate matters in Korea, but nothing came of it.

After Pak's return to Korea, he was constantly under police surveillance. His son urged him to flee to Manchuria but he refused. 'No,' he said to his son, 'I'm working for the Korean Church and must stay.' He said he wanted to be a martyr 'for Jesus, for the Gospel, and for the Korean Church.'

Eventually he was imprisoned in 1941 on the charges of opposing the law for the control of religions, and of 'lèse majesté'. He died in the Pyenyang penitentiary on March 13, 1945, at the age of 70.

In the same penitentiary Pastor Choi Sangnim, a joyful Christian of whom we cannot now speak, died two months later. There were 21 Christians whose names are known, imprisoned in Pyengyang in the summer of 1945. Most of them had been held in this vermin-infested jail for around five years. They went through court examinations but were never formally declared guilty. Nevertheless police records are said to have been found at the close of World War II showing that the Japanese authorities planned to execute them in the last desperate months of the war and only the actual surrender of Japan on August 15, 1945, seems to have saved them.

MISS AHN YOUNGAE

Miss Ahn Youngae was a servant girl from north Korea. As a Christian working for a Japanese family who took her with them to Manchuria, she became more and more troubled by the task of having to put a portion of the daily rice before the god-shelf, a task required by her employer. At first she would secretly spit on the rice to show her disdain and disapproval of what she was doing, but this did not seem a very worthy or clear testimony, so she finally decided to give up her job. She was a good worker and the Japanese employer was loath to lose her. Claiming that she owed him for transportation to Manchuria, and in other ways, he tried to hold on to her, but in vain.

She later found employment with us. When working for us, she shared a rented room, near the Korean church in the Chinese part of the city, with the Bible Woman of the church, Mrs Kim Sinbok, a young widow with an excellent testimony and a cheerful disposition.

When many of the leaders were being rounded up by the police, Mrs Kim was arrested for her opposition to shrine worship. Some days later Miss Ahn took to the jail a change of clothing, a Bible, and toilet paper (the absence of which was not one of the least of the hardships of oriental prison life), hoping to give them to Mrs Kim. The police seized the opportunity to question her about her connection with Mrs Kim, and about her attitude towards shrine worship. She had not been a leader, just a humble church member, but when she replied that she believed shrine worship to be idolatry, she too was imprisoned.

Almost a year later, the Christians in the Harbin Presbyterian Church (Manchuria), of which she was a member, were told that she was being released because she was dying. They found the girl, who had always been meticulous about her person and appearance, completely broken. Her hands and neck were black from months without washing. She had suffered from typhus. Her hair, uncombed for months, was matted, with lice visibly crawling over it. Her face was thin and wasted. Her lips were broken out with sores, her little hands mere skeletons. She could hardly talk. Only her luminous eyes seemed to speak. Painfully she gasped the story of her sufferings, but mostly telling of the victories the Lord had given her. She had had her Bible much of the time. I have it now, with the pages creased, as Koreans do, where she folded them back to mark verses that had especially helped her.

She lingered almost a month after her release from prison, too weak to hold and read her Bible, almost too weak to pray, denied strength for the hearty singing which used to mean so much to her. What I especially noticed was that she had times of discouragement, or of being offended because of lack of attention, or of being forgotten by friends or loved ones. I even heard a Christian once question her faith for these reasons. But when I saw her face relax as I read God's Word to her, or saw a tear roll slowly down her cheek at the singing of a loved hymn, or heard her faint but fervent amens to my prayers, there was no doubt in my mind about her faith. I only realized, as I had never realized before, that the devil has no mercy, and does not even leave the 'brand snatched from the burning' to die in peace. He tempts and torments to the very end. I began to realize then, more deeply, what it means to 'endure to the end' and to seek to prepare *myself* to be faithful 'to the end'.

In spite of loving and skilful medical and nursing care at the hands of Dr and Mrs (also an M.D.) Roy M. Byram, and their staff, Youngae ('Eternal Love') continued to fail. One morning, Dr Byram, on his usual rounds stopped by Youngae's bed. For some reason, he was led to talk about heaven and its glories. He had not been gone from the ward many minutes when Miss Kim, the nurse's aid, whose brother was at that time in prison and would himself later die a martyr's death, rushed from the ward to say Youngae had died. She said that, shortly after Dr Byram left the ward, Youngae had gathered all the strength in her wasted body to cry 'Abba-jee ap-hu-ro kam-nee-da' ('I'm going into the presence of my Father') and died.

The Christians buried her in the Russian cemetery, and on the stone was engraved in Korean and Chinese characters, which can be read by educated people of Korea, China or Japan, the verse in Revelation 12:11: 'They overcame him because of the blood of the Lamb, and because of the word of their testimony; and they loved not their life even unto death'.

EVANGELIST LEE YONGHEE

Evangelist (lay-preacher) Lee Yonghee had been a young elder, a solid businessman in a very large church in Sin Weejoo, on the northern border of Korea. He left his business and moved with his large family into North Manchuria to do pioneeer evangelism. He worked primarily among the Korean farmers flocking into the country to settle areas being developed by Japanese or Korean companies as semi-co-operative farms. He was a cheerful, tireless, efficient worker. In a matter of a few years he had seven little country congregations started.

As the shrine question became more acute in both Korea and Manchuria (by that time occupied by the Japanese), he found himself driven to take an open stand against shrine worship, and began, positively, to teach and instruct his people against it. When children from his churches and Sunday schools refused to worship shrines at the 'farm grammar schools,' it created an unpleasant problem of discipline. Conditions in Manchuria were similar to those of the early days in the western United States. Bandit raids were frequent. Japanese army mop-up squads were sent hither and yon to deal with them. The people were often caught between the two horns of trying to buy off their lives by appeasing raiding bandits, on the one hand, and resisting the army's ruthless extermination of whole families, groups or even villages who collaborated with the bandits, on the other. Blood flowed easily and life was cheap. It was well to keep on the best possible terms with the Japanese government, which was the rising power in Manchuria at the time, and, more especially, with the fanatical military leaders.

One winter, a Japanese mopping-up expedition was stationed in the country town where Mr Lee had a church. Their objective was to clean out the bandits in the area. The soldiers had been there several months without success, and were about to leave. By a clever ruse, the non-Christian Principal of the local school, helped the soldiers to surprise and annihilate the whole bandit band. At the drinking party celebrating this victory and honouring the Principal for his part, the Principal unburdened himself to the Japanese officer about his troubles with the Christians. The officer blustered, 'Kill those who oppose you, or drive them out of here, and you will have our backing.' Emboldened by such words, the Principal began to threaten the Christians and especially evangelist Lee. The Christians were told that if either evangelist Lee or I, the missionary in charge of the area, should set foot in the village, we would be killed. The Christians therefore wrote letters and even sent messengers, urging us not to come. In spite of these threats, evangelist Lee sent word that he would make his regular round of the churches, and I felt I dare not be less bold, and accompanied him. We went together when we visited this church for the first time after these threats. We faced the possibility of ambushment and feared that we were seeing the light of day on earth for the last time. But nothing came of the threats, except our flushing a herd of five deer trying to find food under the snow beside our path. Their jumping up frightened us more than it did them, I am sure.

On another occasion evangelist Lee went to the railroad station to see and express his sympathy for a Bible Woman who had been arrested and was being taken back to Korea under police guard. For contacting her, he himself was handcuffed there on the spot and taken along to the train. Like Peter, I followed afar off and shared his joy when, as the train started to move, they released him.

Evangelist Lee's boldness seemed to be honoured by the Lord. For some reason the authorities seemed almost afraid to touch him. Christians being sought by the police for their stand against shrine worship in Korea fled to Manchuria and found refuge in remote country areas, and Mr Lee's churches sheltered many of these refugees. But evangelist Lee was not content. He felt he must go back to the big churches in Korea and urge them to take a stronger stand against shrine worship. I wondered if looking after his own parishes was not good enough and suggested that he should 'leave well alone', but, for evangelist Lee, the situation in Korea was not 'well' and he made his trip.

Of course, pulpits were closed to him, so he held cottage meetings in the homes of those dissatisfied with the way things had gone in the church, being welcomed in one cottage group after another. The police got wind of his activities and it was while he was holding one of these meetings that the place was surrounded by police. An officer entered and ordered evangelist Lee to come out, whereupon he called for a hymn to cover the interruption of the meeting. The police on the outside, not used to congregational singing, thought a riot had broken out and, leaving their posts, rushed into the house. Most of those gathered were given an opportunity to escape by the different doors and windows, but evangelist Lee himself and several others were arrested. Evangelist Lee died in prison.

His great text had been 'He that endureth to the end, the same shall be saved'. The words of his text, 'to the end', and the peculiar emphasis he put on them, were lovingly mimicked and became almost a battle cry among the Christians – 'Gut Kajee!' ('To the end').

EVANGELIST PAK EEHUM

Evangelist Pak Eehum was born in 1910 in North Pyengan Province. After graduating from grammar school he gained himself the equivalent of a high school education by reading and self-development. This was recognized when he later enrolled and graduated from the Bible Institute in Sin Weejoo, on the northern border of Korea.

In 1939, he was one of 30 men who secretly met with

Pastor Choo Kichul the martyr, after his release from his first imprisonment, and pledged themselves to stir all Korea, and work for the abolition of shrine worship 'to the end, even if it meant death'.

The constant harassment of the police became so unbearable that evangelist Pak fled to Manchuria. I met him at that time. In spite of his limited formal education, he had held a government job for some years before entering Bible Institute, and his native wit and ability, together with his life as a public official, had themselves served to give him a degree from the 'University of Hard Knocks'. When I met him, he was a furtive fugitive, a sharp, clever-speaking bundle of energy.

There were two things especially characteristic of evangelist Pak at this time. On the one hand, he was usually strong and sharp in the things he said and did about shrine worship. If his hearer did not agree or heed after one or two admonitions about the sin of shrine worship he would sharply turn from him, sometimes even while eating at the same table, later not even greeting him if they should pass on the street. This was in accordance with his understanding of 2 John 10, Romans 16:17, and 1 Corinthians 5:11. During the years of World War II this practice was followed by many, loosely tied together through their common stand against shrine worship. At the end of the war, they emerged as the Chai-gun-Pah, or Reconstruction Group. They would have no fellowship with people in what they called the 'present-day Church', calling them children of the devil, and their church buildings 'devils' shrines'.

The other characteristic of evangelist Pak was that, in spite of his urging such an uncompromising stand, he also advised people to flee, rather than fall into the hands of the police. He used evangelist Kim Yoonsup as an example, a man who at that time had been in prison eight times for his opposition to shrine worship and had finally given in to the Japanese. Pak would declare, 'You cannot hold out if you once fall into their hands, so just keep out of their hands.' This advice was not easy to take in the case of women tied down with families or others equally tied to some geographic location. In line with his own advice, Pak refused to accept salaried leadership of any local church, lest he be tied down. He kept moving about Manchuria, and later about North China, stirring up Christians to a strong stand.

The police finally arrested him in North China in 1940, as one of the more-than-seventy 'death pact band' members. He was tortured more than many others, one of the most painful practices being to drive bamboo splints into his fingers under his finger nails. Under torture he would cry 'Hallelujah to the Name of the Lord' and 'How am I worthy?'

The spoiled corn and beans that were part of prison fare during the war years helped to impair his health. He was one of fourteen members of the same group who were eventually brought to trial on February 3, 1942. The remainder of the seventy, mostly laymen, had been previously released for one cause or another, a few by compromising.

Evangelist Pak was given 12 years' hard labour in prison, almost the severest sentence received by any one of the fourteen. But he died in the Mukden (Manchuria) penitentiary in 1943, a year after receiving his sentence. In his death he proved that he had been wrong in saying 'You cannot hold out once you fall into their hands'. Rather he found the words of his Saviour true – 'My grace is sufficient for you', and 'He will give you a way of escape'.

14 : The Witness of Evangelist Kim Yoonsup

EVANGELIST KIM YOONSUP WAS BORN IN THE village of In-doo in Syenchun County of North Pyengan Province. He was brought up in a non-Christian home and was known as one of the 'bad boys' of the village. But when he was about twenty years old he became a Christian. After experiencing regeneration, his life was filled with 'much grace', according to Elder Chung Bongsung, one who later shared imprisonment with him, and to whom I am indebted for filling in many of the details of Yoonsup's life.

Kim had two years beyond grammar school in formal secular education. Following his baptism, he entered the North Pyengan Presbytery's Bible Institute and led services in a small country church until his graduation.

After graduation, he gave himself to full-time work for the Lord and pioneered churches in Duk-in and Wul-wha villages, helping to carry the stones himself for the first little chapel at Duk-in. The grace of the Lord was upon him and the work prospered wherever he went. He was large, over six feet tall, healthy, had a good voice and was in demand as a leader in the churches of the area.

When the Assembly of the Korean Presbyterian Church yielded to government pressure and formally declared that shrine worship was not idolatry, but merely a patriotic act, Kim was greatly disturbed in his mind and preached a strong sermon entitled, 'Daniel's Purposed Aim', which greatly moved the hearts of the hearers. The police got wind of his preaching, and detectives in his audience re-

ported the things he said. As a result he was arrested and
exposed to various kinds of torture, one being the famed
'water cure', in which the prisoner is stretched out, face
upwards, on a narrow bench, hands tied under the bench,
head hanging down over the end of the bench. Water is
then poured from a kettle down his nostrils, practically
drowning him. Sometimes red pepper is added to the water
as a special refinement of the torture. At another time, Kim
was branded with a hot iron. On one occasion, he told me,
several police seized him and, using the back of a chair as
a fulcrum, tried to bend his rigid body in a bow toward
the shrine in the corner of the police station, thinking that
if they could make him bow, even against his will, he would
feel compromised and weaken. But Kim, being tall and
strong, resisted vigorously, lying on the floor and kicking
like a baby. He was kicked in the head and body and his
clothes torn, but he still refused to bow, and they seemed
unable to make him do so.

At other times the police resorted to kindly talk, and
sought to reason him into bowing. 'Christianity was a western religion' and westerners were not as strict about keeping God's commandments as they expected orientals to be,
or even as demanding as Kim was of himself, they argued.
Also many Christians, including some missionaries and
ministers, saw nothing wrong in Shinto worship. Even the
General Assembly of the Presbyterian Church, the leaders
of the Seventh Day Adventist Church, and the Vatican itself, had approved of it. Did he think he was the only good
Christian in the world?

But whether it was torture or argument or blandish-
ments, Kim met each testing with prayer for strength and
wisdom and with God's Word. Perhaps the most difficult
form of temptation was freedom itself. When the authorities

were not able to break him in other ways, they gave him up as a hopeless case and released him, but at the same time warning him that he would be arrested again if he continued to teach as before. As with the apostles in Acts 4 : 17, it was a case of 'let us threaten them and let them go'. How precious freedom is after imprisonment! But, for Kim, it could be had only at the price of keeping his mouth shut. Only one who has been through such a trial (and the writer speaks from experience) can know the strength of such a temptation to silence. But Kim did not yield to the temptation. On his release, he continued preaching as before. He was arrested again. The torturing was more severe. This arrest-and-release policy was repeated until he had been imprisoned eight times.

It was while in prison for his eighth time that Kim broke. This all happened before I ever met him. I have read and even heard, from such men as evangelist Pak, several accounts of Kim's compromise, in which they say that it came about under pressure of torture, water-cure, branding and so forth. Such reports are liable to discourage Christians and make them feel, 'If a man like Kim finally broke, dare I think I could hold out?' Even before I met Kim, I used to doubt the validity of the 'lesson' people drew from Kims' compromise, namely, 'You had better not fall into the hands of the police. Flee! You won't be able to hold out any more than Kim did'. God's Word says, 'There hath no temptation taken you but such as man can bear'. I was glad, therefore, when I eventually met Kim and heard from his own lips the true story of his compromise.

He said he had been brought to prison for his eighth time. Prison, torture, even death, were not so hard to endure or face as were the periods of release, when, against what seemed to be common wisdom, he must carry on the struggle. It was the times when he would be torn from his wife and children that were hard. His wife bravely encouraged him, but the little four-year-old boy would cry inconsolably when his father was led away again by the police. And so, like Elijah under the juniper tree, he came to the point when he wanted to die.

It was just while he was attempting suicide that the guard called him from his cell for another period of examination. On all previous occasions, such a summons turned him to the Lord for strength and wisdom, and the Lord sustained him. He told me that sometimes, under the severest torture, he actually rejoiced in the Lord. But on this occasion it was different. The sin of attempted suicide had broken fellowship with the Lord and such fellowship is not easily or quickly restored. He followed the guard, numb and prayerless of soul. As a matter of form he was again ordered to bow to the shrine, and to the surprise of the police, he meekly obeyed. They were delighted at his change of mind and asked him to put his seal to a statement that it was not idolatrous to bow to a shrine. Again, in a numb way, he submitted. He was now released and told he was free to preach and hold meetings. But like Peter, Kim went out and wept bitterly.

Kim resigned his work as an evangelist and moved to Manchuria. He was not only strong of body but good at mechanics. Before becoming a Christian, he had handled different kinds of machines in his farm village. His family had to live, so he started a rope-making factory, which provided a good living for himself and other Christian fugitives from Korea. But he was not happy. He had a calling from the Lord, and the voices in the church, speaking out against the idolatry of shrine worship, were so few! But what could he do? He had compromised. Furthermore he had sinned wilfully. Was there any forgiveness for him? And under the circumstances, how could he lead others?

He had heard of our work in North Manchuria, and, in his distress, he came to me. It was my privilege to point out to him that 'there is no more sacrifice for sin' – fastings, prayers, nothing whatsoever can be added to what Christ has done. 'He who knew no sin became sin for us', He did it 'once for all', and 'if we confess our sins He is *faithful and just* to forgive us our sins and to *cleanse us from all unrightness*'. It was not a new story to Kim, but it helped to turn his eyes to Jesus *alone*, and in turning he found forgiveness and victory.

He wrote to the police, retracting his signed statement, and subsequently found much liberty in expounding God's Word and in exhorting Christians to stand. He went from place to place strengthening the Christians. He was much in demand. Often, after the close of the regular evening meeting, Christians would gather about him, asking him to give them proof-texts to meet particular phases of the whole shrine problem. Such informal meetings would last far beyond midnight, and no one seemed to get tired; their lives were at stake.

About a month after the writing of his retraction, police came from Korea to arrest him. He was at our home at the time, and when a messenger from his home came, saying they were looking for him, we had prayer together and then he went fearlessly and cheerfully to meet them. And so he was imprisoned for his ninth time. The date was March or April, 1940.

During this imprisonment Kim suffered from dysentery and malnutrition. In December of 1940, shortly after Miss Ahn Youngae had been released only to die, Kim's wife received word to come and remove her husband, as he too was dying and they were releasing him. When she arrived at the prison, she found her husband lying on the frozen ground. His underwear had long since been torn up for bandages with which to bind up the wounds of other prisoners, and his big Korean jacket had slipped up, leaving his bare back against the hard frozen ground. He was too weak even to adjust his clothes to protect himself. She got him home in a Russian taxi.

I did not learn of Kim's release until the next morning. When I arrived at the home, I found him being tenderly cared for, lying on the warm, heated Korean floor. He tried to lift his head, but fell back. He tried to speak, but I could not hear him across the little room. I bent close to him and he uttered the two words: 'Immanuel', 'Hallelujah', *Immanuel*, God with us, and *Hallelujah*, Praise the Lord. His greatest awareness was that God was with him and in his suffering he was praising the Lord!

But that was not the end. He began to improve. Towards Christmas time, the members of the church went together to buy him a warm, fur-lined overcoat. We were having our services in different houses, and, though proscribed by the government, Kim's home was one of the regular meeting places. As Kim got better he led the services in his home, though still having to lean on a big stick to move himself around. I especially recall the communion service which I led there. Christians from our various meeting places had gathered for it. Kim gave the message. Thumbing quickly and familiarly through his big Bible, he brought us a two-hour message on 'Fear not'. 'It's wrong to fear', he declared. He took us through the Scriptures to show why it is wrong to fear, opening up the many promises the Lord gives us for times of danger.

'How do you have the courage to keep going in the face

of constant arrests?' Kim was asked at about this time. 'When I became a Christian, I died with Christ,' was his humble answer, 'and once you are dead, what men do to you cannot hurt you.'

Even on the day of the communion, every knock at the door made us wonder if it was not another call from the police. It was not many weeks after this, early in 1941, that Kim, still leaning on his stick, was arrested for the tenth and last time. It was a time when the authorities arrested about 70 Christians, called by the press 'the death pact band' (Kyul Sa Dan) because of the covenant to which they had subscribed. They were brought from all parts of Manchuria. The press made it appear that a great conspiracy against the government had been uncovered, though we had been quite open in urging subscription to the covenant. While trying to make it appear that the members of the 'Band' were enemy agents disloyal to the government, the press also spoke of them as people who had no awareness of the world about them, as people who were 'looking only for the coming of Jesus on the clouds'.

It was the writer's privilege to be in prison with Kim in the same penitentiary in Antung, Manchuria, between November 22 and December 5, 1941. I saw Kim several times and talked with him briefly, though somewhat indirectly, once. We were both trying to witness to the Korean guard who was watching us. I had told the guard of Kim's many imprisonments for Christ, and that we were both 'in' for the same reasons.

'Aren't you afraid you will die in prison?' the guard asked, for prison conditions were not meant to do more than barely sustain life, and the death of prisoners was not uncommon. I told him that eternal life meant so much to us that, while death was not pleasant to contemplate, it was not such a fearful thing in comparison to the loss of eternal life.

Kim spoke up saying, 'Pastor, I practically died again this time. It was from a case of typhoid fever. I was even unconscious for a time.' Then he added, 'But, Pastor, when you know Jesus, it's cheap to die.' (Chooknan gussi hul hayo).

Kim's sanity and lack of fanaticism impressed me on one particular occasion during our imprisonment in Antung together. One of our fellow Christians, Choi Hanki, had lost his mind under the torture. Strangely enough, the guards had called Mrs Roy Byram and myself from our cells to pray with him, possibly, like Herod, hoping to see some miracle. Choi had been an attractive young evangelist with a wife and two lovely children. I was shocked when I saw him, broken in mind, sitting slumped in a chair, his clothes disarranged, his wrists tied with leather thongs to a great leather belt around his waist so he could not hurt himself. His eyes were like those of a wild animal. Mrs Byram and I had prayer for him there in the prison dispensary and then were taken back to our respective cells. What I had seen kept haunting me. I could not get Choi and his family out of my mind. As I prayed for him the verse kept recurring to me, 'This kind can come out by nothing, save by prayer and fasting'. In spite of the fact that prison fare always left me hungry, I determined to set aside a day for fasting and prayer. Through one of our inter-cell contacts, I suggested that Kim, who had done much prayer and fasting before imprisonment, should join me. He sent word back that his body was greatly weakened (it being his tenth imprisonment) and he would join me in prayer for Choi, but that he felt he must conserve his strength for whatever lay ahead, so he would not fast. This rejoiced me more than if he had agreed to fast. Choi, it should be added, was released within a week and later recovered sanity and was being greatly used of the Lord in North Korea when last heard of before the Communists completely clamped down on the church.

Kim with thirteen other Christians was finally brought to trial in January 1942. The charges against them were the same as those made against the prisoners in Korea: violating the public peace; lèse majesté (treason); irreverence; and giving aid to the enemy.

Kim was recognised by the authorities as the leader. The judges questions were mostly addressed to him. His fellow prisoners, including Pak Eehum, who was himself quite outstanding, recognised the firm but gentle Kim as their spokesman.

On the first day of the trial, the judge said to Kim, 'According to your beliefs, if a man serves any god except your Jehovah God he will be cast into hell; do you then believe that His Majesty the Emperor who serves the gods of his ancestors will go to hell?'

'Yes, he will' (Hai, soo desu), Kim replied.

'Do you really mean it?' the judge asked, (his eyes wide as saucers and his face red with anger', according to Elder Chung Bongsung, one of the fourteen being tried).

'Do you mean it?' (Hontoka), the enraged judge repeated for the third time.

Without hesitation, but with a prayer in his heart, Kim answered, 'Yes, he will.' Despite his boldness, he seemed calm and relaxed.

The trial was not over in one or two days. It ran on for ten days. Gradually the atmosphere in the court room changed. The grace of the Lord seemed to be on His servants as, with the help of the Holy Spirit, they gave their

strong testimony. As the trial proceeded, the judges themselves became more 'strained', as though they were the ones
who were on trial. The Lord provided a 'gracious atmo-
phere' making the court become more like a church, with
Kim preaching the Word of God, Elder Chung said. He
also reported that the prisoners were made to remember the
words of the Lord in Matthew 10: 18–20: 'It shall be
given you in that hour what ye shall speak, for it is not ye
that speak, but the Spirit of your Father which speaketh
in you.'

On the last day but one of the trial, two of the fourteen
gave in, and agreed to shrine worship – Kim Choongdo a
public school teacher who was given 'eight years', and
evangelist Kim Kyungduk who was given 'twelve years'.
The others felt, on the one hand, the grim agony 'of this
break in their ranks and at the same time were moved to
tears of thankfulness for the grace of God without which
they knew they themselves could not stand.'

Following the preliminary summing up of the case, all
fourteen were moved from the big common cells where
they had been held, to the block of smaller cells, usually
reserved for 'foreign prisoners', the very cells where Dr
Byram of the Independent Board for Presbyterian Foreign
Missions and I had been held for a month and a half, just
a few months prior to this. Kim Kyungduk, after yielding,
sobbed pitifully all night, and declared that on his release
he would withdraw his consent to shrine worship, but does
not seem to have had the courage to do so.

On the last day of the trial, when the prisoners were
brought from their respective cells and were waiting in the
basement of the court house to be led into the court room,
evangelist Kim Yoonsup said to his fellow prisoners:
'Brothers, since we have reached the end of the road, the

opportunity further to admonish or reprove others is past. Every one is free. As we are at the fork in the road of life and death, those who would die for Jesus will die together, and those who would live will do as they wish. But there is one thing to remember, the mouths of the lions which wanted to swallow Daniel were only open mouths; they could not actually eat Daniel, could they?' These words were a great strength to his friends. Thus evangelist Kim helped the others and was like a general commanding troops on the front line. When evangelist Pak Eehum spoke of him admiringly as 'general', Kim Yoonsup with his characteristic faith and humility said that he could not be general, 'Jesus is our General.'

During the noon recess of the preceding day, after two of the men had capitulated, the prisoners were all sent back to the cells in the court house basement and given their usual cake of steamed corn-meal. The cells are built around the walls, facing inward, with an open space in the middle, so that the guard, sitting in this space can keep an eye on all the prisoners. The occasion was fraught with emotion. It was drawing to the close of a long struggle. Though each ate his or her corn-cake in a separate cell, they did so in a kind of circle about the open space. With charges having been pronounced against them, the prisoners felt bound together as never before, and their noon meal became a kind of 'sacrament' of the Lord's body. Kim, the spokesman, referring to it, said, 'The Lord has, as it were, prepared for us His holy meal, how good is this time!' What added poignancy and heightened the meaning of the 'communion' was that just as they bowed their heads in prayer and were about to eat, for some reason, the two men who had recanted were called out by the guards, and had to leave their meal untouched. This strange differentiation between the two and the twelve occurred again on the following and last day. The sentences had been pronounced. The court had kindly allowed friends and relatives to buy dishes of 'domburi', (a rice, meat and egg, one-dish-meal, common in Japan) for each of the prisoners, before they started serving their long sentences. Again, just as they were about to eat, the two who had recanted were called from the room and had to leave the food they so craved, untouched. Kim said, 'This is the supper the Lord has provided and He has not allowed those to join us who have refused to take this stand of separation from idols with us.'

The following are the names of the 12 who were finally sentenced on February 3, 1942, and the terms to which they were sentenced:

Kim Yoonsup	Evangelist	15 years
Pak Eehum	Evangelist	12 ,,
Chun Bongsung	Evangelist and Elder	10 ,,
Kim Yangsoon	Evangelist	10 ,,
Sin Okyuh	Bible Woman	10 ,,
Kim Sinbok	Bible Woman	10 ,,
Pak Myungsoon	Bible Woman	8 ,,
Han Soochan	Deacon	8 ,,
Chun Choonduk	Deacon	8 ,,
Kim Ungpil	Deacon	8 ,,
Kim Taikyung	Nurse (Deaconess)	8 ,,
Chun Choisun	Yungsoo (Church leader)	6 ,,

As the tide of World War II turned against the Japanese, free civilians were so restricted, and rationing so strict that the whole country became like a vast concentration camp, and the life of criminals in the penitentiaries proportionately difficult. The twelve prisoners were moved from the Antung penitentiary to Mukden.

Kim was skilful with machinery and could have received preferential treatment as a 'technician' but because it meant Sabbath work he chose rather to be an ordinary labourer and worked in the print shop. The guards respected him and he had a great influence among the prisoners. Two robbers from Youngchun in North Pyenyan Province, who had received seven-year sentences, were led to the Lord by Kim. They prayed and studied their Bibles with him and upon their release proved the sincerity of their Christian profession. Some details of Kim's last days were learned through them.

At one time, a Japanese prisoner appeared to be converted through Kim's preaching, but he in turn tried to weaken Kim in his stand. This proved to be a severe testing of Kim's faith. He wondered later whether the Japanese prisoner had not been purposely 'planted'; for when Kim refused to change his stand, the Japanese turned against him, speaking ill of him.

As long as he lived, Kim encouraged his fellow sufferers and constantly challenged them to more saintly living by his own words and life. The prison fare was 'not one fifth' what a man of his size and energy would want, 'if he ate it all', but he used to divide his food 'not only with his friends but with others'. 'He did not stop praying, singing, or witnessing in prison, and became known as a "man of God".'

In his struggle for truth he was bold as a lion, but in his dealing with those about him he was humble and merciful so that even from the lips of one of the Japanese guards was wrung the tribute to his saintliness, 'Anatawa Kami-sama desu' (You are a god).

Hard labour and lack of nourishment following on the tortures and sickness during the more than two years of imprisonment before his trial began to tell. His lungs became affected, and at last, too weak to work in the print shop, he was sent to the prison infirmary.

He was now cut off from any contact with his fellow Christians. The loss of his buoyant leadership was described as having a 'suffocating' effect on them. Only occasional news of him leaked through the infirmary walls, by way of other patients hospitalized for shorter periods. Thus his last days were spent wholly among non-Christians and it was through the lips of non-Christians who were near him and saw him at the time, that we know of his death. In bed he continued to witness to all – prisoners, jailers, and clerks. Those who were there always spoke of him with pity and admiration and were sure he had gone to the heaven of which Christians speak.

For three or four days before his death he kept singing hymns, with a beaming face, like an angel, and repeating, 'It's time for some one from my home to come.' His singing could be heard by well-nigh a thousand prisoners awaiting trial in the floors above and below the infirmary. Listening in the tomb-like silence of the prison, they would, in spite of regulations, occasionally break into applause.

On the last morning, May 3, 1943, when Kim received his morning meal, he divided it carefully into four parts as usual, ate two parts himself, gave the other equally divided parts to two other patients, then fell back in final and peaceful sleep. He had served only fifteen months of his fifteen-year sentence, a month for a year.

The song sung so much during those last days seems to have been the Korean translation of the 'Glory Song',

> *When all my labours and trials are o'er*
> *And I am safe on that beautiful shore,*
> *Just to be near the dear Lord I adore*
> *Will through the ages be glory for me.*

> *O, that will be glory for me! Glory for me!*
> *Glory for me!*
> *When, by His grace, I shall look on His face,*
> *That will be glory, be glory for me!*

His last act of sharing, followed by the peaceful passing in sleep, graphically sealed to the non-Christians among whom he died the testimony concerning his hope of heaven and joy in seeing the Saviour, concerning whom he had been singing so much during his final days.

15 : The Struggle with Communism

EXCEPT FOR THE BURNING OF A WHOLE CHURCH full of Christians in Suwon, and other violence connected with the putting down of the Independence Movement in 1919, in which, as we have seen, a number of Christians participated and suffered, the Japanese did not engage wilfully in the execution of Christians. Among the 50 or more who died under Japanese persecution, I know of none who was executed outright. Christians were imprisoned and tortured, and death came as a result of torture, malnutrition, exposure, disease and illness in prison, not execution. The martyrdoms under Communism, however, were quite different.

When I asked Rev Kim Sangdoo, who spent four years in prison under the Japanese and was once arrested and beaten by members of 'the People's Army' (communists), if there was any difference between Japanese and communist persecution, he put into words what I had come to conclude from the cases I had studied or heard about. The Japanese deal with you strictly on the basis of their laws, while the communists' persecution is 'Moojee' – unprincipled, stupid, and brutal, although on the surface, the communists too hold a semblance of keeping the law.

One evangelist, now an ordained minister, who lived under them for four years, says opposition to Christianity was not direct. In fact, according to another minister from North Korea, church attendance and church membership actually increased during the first three years of communist occupation. The church also seemed to grow in spirituality. Between 1948 and 1950, as the pressure increased, members decreased but the spiritual life of the Christians seemed to deepen. 'If a man stood up for his rights,' the above-mentioned evangelist said, 'he was often let alone, openly.' The words to be underscored in these remarks, however, are the words 'direct' and 'openly'. The same man showed that the indirect and hidden opposition to Christianity was constant and eventually devastating. Ministers might be arrested on some non-religious pretext, and then be released in what would appear to be an act of fair-minded benevolence. But hardly were they out of prison before they would be set upon and brutally killed by a frenzied mob. In a society so completely controlled such killings could not be interpreted as being carried out under anything but the direct orders of the same 'fair-minded, benevolent authority'. Or again, while the church was theoretically allowed to exist (for the communist constitution allows 'freedom of religion'), ministers were often called from their homes for the most innocent reasons, as though 'just for a minute', never to be seen or heard from again. Except when a minister was being cut down brutally, without mercy, by an unprincipled, raw, physical force, he was not often allowed knowingly to meet his real opponent. And even here, brute force was often not the real opponent. In such disappearances, friends did not know the charges against the people. They were not given opportunity to speak in defence of those taken away, and the fate of those who were taken away, while uncertain, had all the marks of finality.

When the United Nations forces freed Korea from Japan in 1945, the Koreans naturally expected that they would have a hand in forming their own government. During 35 years of Japanese occupation, political parties had not been able to function openly, if at all. Now, everyone seemed to come forward with his own political party. While the Christians were not a political party, as such, in this time of transition, they were perhaps as united ideologically as any group in society, by their common faith. The leadership and popularity of the many Christians also made them natural candidates for political leadership. Then, too, many Christian citizens, who had not felt like participating even in the lower brackets of government open to them under the Japanese, because such positions under a pagan government involved compromise, now hopefully stepped forward. They were anxious to see their country built on patterns of government which they had admired from a distance in Christian nations. At first, they seemed naively unaware of the incompatibility of their kind of national aspirations with the aspirations of the communist powers which had been given 'temporary' authority over their country to accept Japan's surrender north of the 38th parallel in Korea and Manchuria.

For a time, the occupying communist forces helped to keep alive the Korean illusion that a government, freely chosen by people with Christian motives and ideals, could still be enjoyed within a communist political framework. The Presbyterian elder, Cho Mansik, known by Koreans as a true patriot and lover of his country, the people's choice, was allowed to head the government under the Russian occupying forces. Non-Christians flocked to the church, which was revived beyond the Christians' expectations.

The church was stronger in North Korea than in any other part of the country, and Christians had held many of the places of responsibility in society, education, health, business and manufacture. Christians were naturally active, therefore, in trying to mould the destinies of their 'liberated' country. One witness said that the responsibility of government was mostly given to ministers, elders, and deacons, at least in Whanghai Province. This may be somewhat of an exaggeration, but points at least to a time of comparative freedom for the church.

When international communism, taking advantage of the military authority that had been given to the Russian army in North Korea, began to extend its purposes of world domination into Korea, the Korean Christians woke up to find themselves aligned against an implacable foe. At first they had regarded communism as a rightful and normal expression of the political aspirations of Christian citizens. On the other hand, by the Communist, Christianity was interpreted as a political crime, an act of vilest rebellion against the state, 'the people', and therefore deserving of the severest punishment, even death.

The first conflict between the church and the communists seems to have broken out on the northern border of Korea in the town of Sin Wiju. Under the leadership of two outstanding Presbyterian pastors, Rev Yoon Hayung and Rev Han Kyungchik, a Christian Social Democratic party was organized in September 1945, immediately following Korea's liberation after World War II. Branches were organized throughout the area. On November 16, 1945 when a 'local' was being organized in Yong Am Po, communists incited labourers in a nearby factory to break up the meeting. In the fight that ensued, a Presbyterian elder was killed on the spot and many were injured. The church building was destroyed and damage was done to the home of Deacon Chang Wonbong, the president of the 'local', and other officers. A few days later, as a result of the feelings aroused over this bloody communist interference in a political meeting, 5,000 students demonstrated before the communist 'People's Government' headquarters, telling them to leave. Korean communists turned machine-guns on the unarmed students while Russians machine-gunned them from the air. Fifty were killed or wounded and eighty, including officers of the Christian Democratic Party, were imprisoned.

In the spring of 1946, many churches planned services to commemorate their first 'Independence Day' since liberation from Japan. March 1, 1919, was the day on which the Koreans had made public a 'Declaration of Independence'. As we observed in earlier pages, 15 of the 33 signers of that Declaration had been Christians, and the part of the Christians in the Independence Movement was well known. The communists did not want to lose the propaganda advantage of the day and planned their own meetings, forbidding the churches to hold these commemoration services.

In spite of arrests, the Christians went forward with their plans. Spontaneous demonstrations broke out in the streets of Pyengyang and other cities which were forcibly put down. In Wiju a communist mob entered a church, wrecked the pulpit, and dragged the pastor around the city on an ox-cart with insulting placards hung about his neck.

In Sansungjin, Manchuria, 48 elders were arrested by the Russian military authorities and then released. Later they were seized, tried by a 'people's court', evidently at the instigation of the same authorities, and killed. One who had been beaten and left for dead survived and eventually escaped to South Korea. The usual 'crimes' charged against people by the communists (in order of heinousness) were:

1 Having been acquainted with Americans,

2 Having held a government office under the Japanese or Republic of Korea government,

3 Having been men of means,

4 Being Christians,

5 Being intellectuals.

As can be seen, there were political overtones in most of these earlier clashes. Some Christians, especially the Reconstruction (Chaigun) Church and the Re-established (Poku) Church people were against such political activity on the part of Christians and they felt the Christians brought persecution on themselves. But none, not even those who were opposed to Christians taking such a lead in politics, would deny for a minute that the communists wanted to bring the church under their complete control for their own purpose.

While it too had its political overtones, the first clash where the Christians were united was the Sunday issue raised in connection with the puppet election set for Sunday, November 3, 1946. A meeting of the five Presbyteries in North Korea was called on October 22, 1946, to decide what to do about it. They made the following declaration in the name of the '2,000 congregations and 300,000 church members':

1 Keeping the Sabbath day holy is of the life of the church, so there should be no attendance upon things other than worship on the Lord's Day.

2 Government and religion should be kept separate.

3 Respect for God in the church building is the proper duty of the church, so that the use of the church building for purposes other than worship is forbidden.

4 In the event that an acting church officer enters the field of politics, he must resign his office in the church.

5 The church stands for freedom of religion and assembly.

The Reconstruction (Chaigun) and Re-established (Poku) Churches, while not parties to this action, had already been standing for these five points, so except for those completely under the communists' thumb the Presbyterians, at least, were agreed.

The communist reaction to the Christians' refusal to vote on Sunday varied in different localities. In some places it was ignored altogether, in others the pressure was severe. Many ministers were arrested and nothing more was heard of them. Elders, deacons, and laymen were imprisoned for one, two, or three months, and then released.

In Chinnampo, Rev Kim Tukmo was condemned to death by a 'people's court' for opposing the Sunday elections and urging his congregation not to vote. Another minister, Rev Yoo, pleaded for his life, using the argument of expediency, that such an act would cause an unfavourable reaction among the people and even world opinion. Kim's life was spared at the time but later both he and Yoo, who defended him, were imprisoned and there has been no further news of them.

In Syenchun the Christians had refused to vote on Sunday but nothing was done about it until a month later when the ministers were rounded up, tried by a 'people's court' and beaten. Rev Lee Soondo, aged 40, died as a result of these beatings. Lee was physically strong and at first defended himself against the mob which was beating him. The communists then ordered 'Christians' to beat him to death to prove their loyalty to the communist government.

In many places the Christians went to church for daybreak prayer-meetings on November 3 before the polls opened, and stayed there, holding meetings, singing, praying, preaching, until midnight when the polls closed. The communists came to Rev Choi Choonho, asking him to tell his congregation that it would be well if they went to the polls at 11 : 30 at night after the services, but this too he refused. Where church services concluded before midnight, people were taken forcibly from the streets and compelled to vote. Rev Lee Chanyoung, now in Pusan, who was in North Korea at the time, says that, while members of the 'Christian League' and a few weak Christians may have voted, he guesses that two-thirds of the Christians did not participate in the voting.

It was, in fact, the action of the five Presbyteries that seemed to occasion the setting up of the above-mentioned 'Christian League' as a counter-measure by the communists.

Pang Sangsoon, a Presbyterian minister, who had been serving as Kim Ilsung's private secretary, was put at the head of this 'Christian' organization to be used by the communists to bring the church into line. Its programme stated:

1 We give absolute support to Kim Ilsung's (communist) North Korean government.

2 We do not recognize the legitimacy of the South Korean Republic of Korea.

3 The church is to lead the people.

4 Therefore the church should take the lead in the elections (i.e. as conducted by the Kim Ilsung government).

A minister from Whanghai Province told me that a Christian was not actually criminally chargeable if he refused to join the 'Christian League', but his failure to do so meant that he would be listed as an enemy of the government, and life would be made miserable for him in many ways. If possible he would be arrested on some other count of political opposition to the government.

Evangelist Kim Changwhan, born in 1927 in North Pyengan Province, studied theology in Japan, and after Korea's liberation became the outstanding leader and Bible teacher of the Reconstruction (Chaegun) Church in Pyengyang. He opposed some of the extreme views on 'separation' held by many in the Reconstruction Church. When the leader of the 'Christian League' tried to get him to join, hoping to win the support of his prestige, Kim reprimanded him for submitting himself to be a tool of the communists. This was reported to the authorities and Kim was arrested. He died as the result of beatings in 1950. His body was recovered and buried by the Christians.

Evangelist Choo Youngjin, son of the Rev Choo Kichul, a famous martyr under the Japanese, was accosted by a Seventh Day Adventist minister in the 'Christian League,' in front of the communist police box and asked why he had refused to join the League. Choo replied, 'If a layman asked me, I would tell him, but you, a minister, ought to know. All I can say to you is "Repent".' Christians who had yielded to League membership were forbidden by its rules to meet on any day but Sunday and Wednesday, and then at the convenience of and to support the communist programme, but Choo, who refused to recognize its authority or control, kept Bible studies and conferences in session most of the time. But in common with so many others, on August 3, 1950, he was called out from his home 'just for a minute' without any special reason, and since then, nothing has been heard of him.

While membership in the League made one temporarily immune to many pressures, it was useful to you only as long as you were useful to the communists. The story of Rev Kim Iktoo, known to many Westerners as the 'Billy Sunday of Korea', a man known throughout the Korean church from the early days, is one in point. In order to get the support of the Five Presbyteries for the 'Christian League,' Kim Iktoo was first imprisoned during the cold of winter and not given sufficient food because he would not join the League. He was over seventy years of age at the time. After he had suffered for a couple of weeks, Pang, the head of the 'Christian League,' just 'happened' into the jail where Kim was being held and made quite a show of demanding why such an honourable man was being treated in this ignominious fashion. He took Kim home with him, supplied him with nice clothes, fed him well, and then 'convinced' him that co-operation with the communists was more sensible than fighting them. He got Kim to agree to urge the Five Presbyteries to approve of the 'Christian League'. This soft approach worked on the aging minister but when he put the matter before the Five Presbyteries he received no support. The commissioners, however, knowing that to take any adverse action would mean trouble for them then broke up without taking any action at all. My informant said that Kim realized he had made a serious mistake, and returned to Sinchun his home town broken in spirit. However he did not have the strength to withdraw his name from the organization, and remained as nominal head of the Whanghai Province 'Christian League'. But after General MacArthur's landing in Inchon when the communists were retreating, Kim Iktoo was shot to death by communist soldiers in his church.

But this is getting ahead of the story chronologically.

THE CHRISTIAN LIBERAL PARTY

In November 1947 Rev Kim Hwasik and Elder Ko Hankyu organized the Christian Liberal Party centering around the Theological Seminary group in Pyengyang. It was at the time when the United Nations Assembly was planning to discuss the Korean question. Their purpose was to work for the uniting of North and South Korea. The police heard of the proposed organization of this party and on November 19, before it had been able to hold a single meeting, Rev Kim and 39 others involved in the planning of the organization were arrested and have not been heard of since.

OTHER PRESSURES ON THE CHURCH

It was Rev Choi Choonho, a minister who opposed the involvement of Christians in political action on either side, who told me of the various kinds of pressure brought against the church in addition to those mentioned above.

1 Christians, along with others, were constantly called out for public works, especially on Sunday. To obey meant breaking the Sabbath, and the disruption of church services, while to disobey was considered opposition to the government.

2 The people, including Christians, were called together for indoctrination meetings almost daily, but especially on Sundays, with similar results to those just mentioned.

3 Children of Christians found it difficult to enrol in Junior or Senior High Schools if 'Christian' was written on their application forms where religious affiliation was indicated.

If they did get into school, things were made difficult for them. They were frequently called back to school on Sundays. My informant said his daughter was expelled from grammar school for silently praying before beginning her classes, and three or four other children in his Sunday school were expelled from school at the same time for the same reason. He, as pastor, was called to the police station over the matter.

4 The communists often demanded the use of church buildings for their political meetings and for posting their political slogans. Refusal meant persecution for the church. Evangelist Choo Youngjin, whose final disappearance was mentioned above in connection with the Sunday election issue, was one of those who opposed the organizing of anti-communist political parties by Christians and, for the same reasons, refused the use of his church for communist rallies. He was imprisoned one month for refusing to put up a communist poster in his church at Chang Hyun.

THE 'NORTH–SOUTH' KOREAN WAR

The greatest number of deaths among Christians took place during the changing fortunes of the 'North–South' war after June 25, 1950.

The sudden attack of the North Korean communist troops against South Korea caught the South Korean populace wholly without warning. Many Christian leaders, together with missionaries, Roman Catholic as well as Protestant, were caught up in the net of the invading forces, before they had time to flee. There were some 'Christian' leaders whose theological and sociological views were such that they vainly supposed their Christianity could live within the communist framework. Still others felt that, as shepherds, they dare not leave their flocks even though they knew it meant certain death. Herded with military prisoners on death marches to the rear, they shared many of the hardships, certainly the anguish and uncertainty. On the 100-mile death march shared by these civilians in November 1950, one reporter states that people died at the rate of one a mile. On one day alone 21 were shot. Of 738 American prisoners taken in September 1950, only 276 survived. Seventy-six were shot, five died of exposure, and 16 sick and wounded were left in a compound and were never seen again.

Of the 18 Roman Catholic missionaries, whose average age was 65, ten including Bishop Patrick J. Byrne died as a direct result of communist cruelties during or after the death march. The communists constantly refused to allow captive priests and ministers to hold services or give spiritual assistance to the prisoners, violating even the Geneva Convention.

In Seoul, Dr Koh of Severance Hospital, Dr Nam Kung-hyuk, former Professor in the Pyengyang Seminary, Dr Song Changun and other well-known men disappeared at the time of the outbreak of hostilities and have not been heard of since. Rev Chun Insun died in prison at that time. Rev Lee Sungui, one of the Professors of Pyengyang Seminary, was shot.

The Anglican Church's Korea Mission, lost three missionaries. Father Charles Hunt was taken from a bed of sickness and survived captivity only a short time. Sister Mary Clare died in captivity and Father Lee disappeared. He was rumoured to have been shot.

Even after the outbreak of war churches continued to

meet but, of course, the pressure to support the communist war effort was increased.

Evangelist Kim, serving a branch chapel of the Chang Hyun Church, 12 miles from Pyengyang, not only refused to join the communist army but refused to carry a card declaring his military status. For this he was imprisoned, beaten and smothered with a quilt. The Christians recovered his badly swollen body for burial. A Sunday school teacher, Kim Sungchoon, attending the funeral, was strengthened by the example of his witness and himself refused to join the communist army. For this he was imprisoned. On the day before the United Nations troops entered Pyengyang, he was called out and asked again if he would fight for the communists. 'One word and you will live', he was told. When he said he would not fight, he was bound with wire to about 20 other people, including several pastors and elders. Some of the group were non-Christians. One of the pastors was identified as Rev Pang Choonwon. These were taken in a truck by night to an anti-aircraft battery trench, six miles from Soonan, and machine-gunned to death. One of the number helped by a man behind, using his teeth to loosen the wire, freed himself, dropped from the truck, and escaped in the dark to tell the story.

This was the time following General MacArthur's landing at Inchon when very many Christians, along with countless others of the population, were slaughtered in cold blood by the retreating communists. In hundreds of cases, as Dr Arch Campbell says, those who came out of hiding too soon to meet the conquering United Nations troops were summarily shot by the communists who had not yet completely withdrawn.

On the West Coast of Korea, in Yumkwang County of South Chulla Province, one informant reported 40,000 people as killed out of a population of 120,000. Whole villages were wiped out by the retreating communists. Three Presbyterian ministers in this county, Revs Kim Bangho, Kim Chongin, and Won Changkwon were among those killed. In the Yumsan Church Rev Kim Bangho's family of eight was killed at the same time, with the exception of one son. Rev Kim used to tell his parishioners that grace for martyrdom was given by God. Elder Huh of the same church, when faced by the communists, urged them to believe in the Lord Jesus Christ and was killed with a bamboo spear. His wife who had been arrested, then released, begged to die with him and was killed. Over 70 in this one church were killed; some with knives, others had stones tied to their necks and were drowned. In the case of one deacon, the stone slipped out of the rope and he was able to swim away only to be killed with a bamboo spear by communists waiting for him when he came ashore.

In the Yawul Church of the same county, the communists gathered the Christians, including the Sunday school children, into the church and killed them, about 80 people in all.

In Pongsan County of Whanghai Province, the Keidong Presbyterian Church usually had about 180 people attending its regular services. After MacArthur's landing the 'People's Police' ordered the Christians to gather in the church building. My informant, who belonged to a nearby church in the same county, said, 'No one thought of disobeying an order of the communist police.' With the exception of three or four members and the pastor who were out of town at the time, all gathered. The communists set fire to the wooden church building and stood outside to shoot down any who might try to escape. The Christians, evidently realizing that they would die either way made no effort to escape, having decided, as the narrator interpreted their action, 'to die clean'. They united their voices in song until the burning building collapsed over their heads and they were all consumed in the fire.

16 : Three Martyrs: Sohn Yangoon and his two Sons

PERHAPS THE BEST KNOWN AND MOST PUBLICIZED cases of martyrdom under the communists were the deaths of the Rev Sohn Yangoon and his boys, Tongin and Tongsin. Although he did not die under the Japanese, his testimony against Shinto worship was one of the more outstanding ones. I did not include his story in earlier chapters because he did not die until the time of the communists, but it is necessary to tell of his witness against Shinto worship to give the complete picture of his martyrdom and that of his sons.

Born in Koosung Village, Haman County, in South Kyungsang Province on July 7, 1902, he graduated from Middle School in Tokyo in 1923, then entered the South Kyungsang Bible Institute. He was married in 1924 and became an evangelist employed by the Pusan leper colony in 1925. He also pioneered churches in Pangujin, Soosan, Namchang, and Wondong. Going on to the Pyengyang Theological Seminary (Presbyterian) in Pyengyang, he graduated in 1938. It was while a seminary student that he first got into difficulties with the Japanese authorities in the area of South Kyungsang Presbytery over the shrine issue. Upon graduation, he accepted a call to the church in the 'Aeyang Won,' a large leper colony established by the Southern Presbyterian Mission in Yusoo, South Chulla Province. This church had more than a thousand members. It was thought that the authorities would not take much interest in a man ministering to these leper outcasts of society.

Sohn Yangoon was called to the police station, however, when, out of respect to his scruples, the Japanese flag had been removed from behind the pulpit at some special meetings which he was conducting in a church outside the colony. The Japanese had been requiring that Christians bow to the Japanese flag before each worship service. At the police station, Sohn argued that flags flying from a house or a ship were like name-plates for identification and reasoned that bowing to the flag was like bowing to one's name-plate. Also, he said, if bowing to the flag made patriots, then any vicious criminal, polygamist or drunkard could become a patriot by bowing. The police decided to release him at the time, only to arrest him later in 1940. Following the arrest his family was evicted from the manse by the police, but members of his leper congregation secretly took up a collection to help them.

Sohn was held in the Yusoo prison for ten months. For a long time, the only way the family could discover that he was alive was when they took fresh laundry to the jail and continued to receive his soiled clothes in return. Eventually, by paying money, the family was allowed to arrange for him to have certain special foods from the prison kitchen, but this very concession seems to have given rise to a distressing rumour that Sohn had compromised.

Through the kitchen grape-vine, Sohn's wife heard that he was being moved to the penitentiary in Kwangju, the provincial capital, for trial. His guards conveniently turned their backs so that she could get in a few words with him, as he was being held on the station platform, awaiting the train. She reminded him of the words of martyr Choo's wife to her husband, 'If you bow before the shrine, you are not my husband,' then added, 'moreover your soul will be lost.' Sohn assured her that he had not compromised, but urged her to pray for him.

Mrs Sohn moved from the leper colony to Kwangju with the younger children. The older boy, Tongin, got a job in Pusan, working at a factory, making wooden barrels, but when they were leaving the leper colony he told the lepers that he would train for the ministry and come back to serve them in his father's place. When he was later drafted for the Japanese army to fight America, Mrs Sohn scattered the family. She put the second boy, Tongsin, in the Zion orphanage in Pusan, and the two youngest, Tonghui and Tongja in the Ai Rin Won (orphanage) in Kupo near Pusan, then took the oldest boy and fled to the island of Namhae, where they remained in hiding until the end of the war. As the persecution intensified, Tongsin, the second boy, left the Zion orphanage to avoid shrine worship. Not knowing where his mother and brother were hiding, he went to live with six lepers who had abandoned the Yusoo leper colony to get away from compromising shrine worship. They had organized themselves into a little community in a remote area of the Hadong Township in Chinju County. He risked contracting the disease to avoid participation in shrine worship, and remained with them to the end of the war.

In the meantime, Sohn was examined by the Prosecutor of the Kwangju court for eight days. At the end of this time, the Prosecutor followed the usual practice of asking him to put his seal to the record of the examination. Sohn had relied on God's Word in making his answers and refused to sign the record, saying, 'They are God's words and not mine, and I have no right to put my seal to God's words as though they were mine.'

[148]

He was tried on November 1941, and convicted on the usual counts: Violating the public peace; Lèse Majesté; Irreverence; Giving aid to the enemy; and given a year-and-a-half sentence. While the military clique was determined on wiping out any opposition, the civil authorities acted more cautiously. They did not want to antagonize the people and tried to avoid head-on collisions over the shrine issue. When the year-and-a-half was up, the Public Prosecutor, Yoda, called Sohn before him. He asked the prison guard about Sohn's record on co-operating with the prison authorities. The guard replied that Sohn had been a model prisoner and that he had faithfully participated in shrine ceremonies. It is not known for certain whether or not this lie was previously planted in the guard's mouth by Yoda as a face-saving device whereby the Prosecutor would be enabled to dismiss and be freed of a difficult case. Whatever went before between the guard and the Prosecutor, Sohn denied that he had participated in shrine worship. This turn of events infuriated the Prosecutor and he condemned Sohn to the permanent prison for incorrigibles, that is to say, for those who 'held dangerous thoughts', located in Chungju, Choongchung Province, in August, 1943. He remained there until Japan's surrender on August 15, 1945, brought liberation.

After liberation, Sohn returned to his old charge as the pastor of Ae Yang Won leper church in Yusoo. The unusual testimony he had made before the Japanese caused him to be much in demand as a preacher throughout the country during this post-war period of reconstruction. The scattered family was brought together again and the children were enrolled in various schools, trying to make up for the education they had lost when expelled from grammar school for refusing to bow to the Shinto shrines.

Tongin enrolled in the Soonchun Normal School and Tongsin in the Soonchun Middle School. They were making good progress in their studies and also were bearing an active Christian testimony among their fellow students. Like so many Korean students they even dreamed of going later to America for advanced studies. But tragedy hit again.

On the night of September 19, 1948, communists in the Yusoo Constabulary Training Camp, finding themselves part of a 500 troop constituency ordered to sail for Cheju Island to fight communist guerrillas, jumped the gun on a planned nation-wide communist uprising against the government of the Republic of Korea. They shot their Korean officers and took control of the local constabulary, then of the city of Yusoo, following which they occupied the city of Soonchun. A reign of terror followed in which 'enemies of the people' (as communists saw them) were tried before 'people's courts'. The affair was well organized. Arm and headbands, banners, leaflets, and posters shouting communist slogans seemed to spring up with the morning dew on September 20. The premature uprising in one locality saved the rest of the country, but in that locality terror reigned. The Reds spread the lie that Seoul, Taegu, Pusan, and other key cities had fallen to the communists, and that soon all South Korea would be freed from capitalist tyranny.

Whether it was because they had had enough of being fugitives under the Japanese, or whether the communist propaganda had convinced them of the futility of escape, Tongsin and Tongin decided not to flee but to prepare for death, to flee into the bosom of their Heavenly Father. Early on the morning of the 21st, they arose and had prayer together, then they bathed and put on their best clothes. Student friends, knowing the prominent place they had held as Christians in the eyes of their classmates, came to their boarding house urging them to run, but they remained in their room.

At about 10 o'clock, a mob of communist students came and dragged them from their boarding house. They took them to an area behind the government buildings where bodies of other victims of the 'people's court' lay scattered. They reviled and threatened the boys, especially beating Tongin, the elder. Tongsin tried to put himself between them and his brother and the students turned on him.

When rumours of the boys' martyrdom reached the parents, Hong, a leper, volunteered to go into the distressed city and check the reports. He learned from their landlord that the communist students, after dragging the boys away, had ransacked the boys' room and carried away their papers to the Red headquarters. The landlord also heard that the boys had been shot. The leper made a search and finally found their bodies. From a Christian, whose husband had also been shot, he learned that the boys had urged their captors to believe in Jesus and had patiently witnessed until the end came. When Tongin would not deny his faith in Jesus, Ahn Chae Sun, the leader of the communist students, prepared to shoot him with a revolver. Tongsin again tried to put himself between Ahn and his brother, only to be pulled away. Tongin was then blindfolded and shot. Tongsin threw himself on his brother's body and was himself shot.

In two days this local communist revolt was put down and Ahn, the killer of the two boys, was apprehended. Pastor Sohn, hearing that the boy had been seized, sent a pastor friend and his own daughter to plead for the boy's life, offering to adopt the killer of the boys as his own son.

The colonel in charge was so impressed with the request that after contacting Sohn to hear the strange request directly from the father, he turned the boy over to him. Sohn received permission from Ahn's parents to adopt him and witnessed to them and to the boy, later enrolling the boy in the Higher Bible Institute in Pusan. The grateful parents, in turn, asked permission to adopt one of the Sohn girls to live in their home and teach them about Christ, promising to see that she was given a good education.

The violent death of the celebrated minister's two sons, followed by his adopting the killer, was a shock to the whole country. Students were emotionally affected by the story of the two boys and pledged themselves to greater consecration. Pastor Sohn was in even greater demand as a speaker at meetings.

Then the communists poured across the 38th parallel on June 25, 1950. As they over-ran more and more of South Korea the populace fled before them into the little 50-mile perimeter around Pusan bounded by Masan, Taegu, and Kyungju. Rev Sohn was at the leper colony and was warned to flee, but chose to stay with his flock. Many were arrested that summer. Sohn was not arrested until September 13 when he was taken to Yusoo. The jail was so full that he was placed with many others, arrested earlier, in an old grain warehouse until MacArthur's famous Inchon landing. Before retreating on September 28, the communists tied 75 of the prisoners with straw ropes and led them out by night to a place about three miles north of Yusoo and shot them. Their bodies were found the next day.

His previous suffering under the Japanese, the martyrdom of his two sons, followed by his generosity to the killer, and finally his own martyrdom at the hands of the communists, made Sohn's case rather outstanding, but many unpublicized saints suffered and witnessed as faithfully. Sohn and his two sons' martyrdoms have been popularized in a two-volume book written in Korean by the Rev Ahn Yongjun, *The Atomic Bomb of Love*. The book has gone into several editions.*

Besides Pastor Sohn, Mrs Yoon, Bible Woman of the First Presbyterian Church of Yusoo, Mr Kim Unki, President of the Yusoo YMCA, Deacon Huh Sangyong, Deacon Kim Chaisun, all of Yusoo, were among those killed. Rev Cho Sanghak of the Dukyang Church and Chi Hanyung, an older theological student, and two of his sons (one a public school teacher from Ulchon) were among the nine Christians positively identified among the 75 led out for execution at this time.

My informant knew only two of the 75 who escaped death. One was a non-Christian youth, arrested for his political activities in connection with the South Korean government. He had been able, with the help of a prisoner behind him, to wriggle out of the ropes that held him and make his escape in the dark. He was greatly impressed with the conduct of the Christians during those hot summer days of confinement in the crowded warehouse. He especially spoke of Rev Cho Sanghak who had been there since the middle of July. This old pastor had stayed with his flock when the communists invaded, saying, 'What would the communists want to do with a man 73 years old?' The young man said Cho preached, from the day of his arrest, to the hundreds who passed through the warehouse jail that summer. He always asked the blessing over his food in a loud clear voice, remembering in his prayer those imprisoned with him. This was a great comfort to the young

* Including an English version entitled, *The Seed Must Die*, published by Inter-Varsity Press.

man and the other prisoners. The communist guards tried to shut him up but after a brief pause he would speak up again. The guards stretched his mouth with their fingers, tearing his lips. Later one punched him in the mouth with his rifle butt, badly bruising his mouth. Cho preached to guards and judges of the 'people's court' alike. He would continue witnessing though beaten. He expected to die, and seemed to fear nothing.

The other to escape was a high school boy, the younger son of Chi Hanyung, the theological student. At the place of execution the prisoners were called by name, a small group at a time, told to strip and lay their clothes in a pile, then told to step forward and be shot. As the boy laid down his clothes he made a bolt for the hills. The Red soldiers fired after him, but he made his escape in the nude.

When Pastor Cho's body was recovered the next day, they found that he had been shot in the head from the rear. The bullet coming out in his face disfigured him beyond recognition. He had to be identified through other markings.

Rev Han Choonmyung, now Professor in Yonsei College in Pusan, tells of the mass slaughter of close to 300 prisoners from which he himself and six others miraculously escaped. Han served a church near the city of Wonsan on the east coast of Korea. He had seen the same pressures brought to bear on the church that have been described in other areas. Christian children in public schools had been made to criticize themselves. Children's 'People's courts' were set up and Christian children were judged guilty and expelled from schools by their fellow students. Christian teachers refusing to join the communist labour party lost their jobs. Christians not joining the communist party were given a smaller grain ration than those in the party and found their activities blocked at every turn. When they found life unbearable and reluctantly decided they would have to leave their centuries-old ancestral homes for South Korea, this was interpreted as being an act of treason and they were often imprisoned or exiled to forced labour camps. Christians were sometimes arrested, then released on condition that they became informers against their pastors and other Christians. Han said that three different members of his congregation showed him forms they had been given on which to make such reports. He said that whenever a stranger appeared in the congregation, the deacons would slip word to the pastor to be cautious of what he said in case the stranger might be a communist spy.

In 1949 a group of ministers and elders in Wonsan attempted to set up an organization to work with the Republic of Korea government in case the 38th Parallel was removed. This was discovered and Rev Kwon Uibong (Chairman), Elder Pak Changheun, and a high school teacher, Chang Choosoo, were arrested and sent to do hard labour in Hamheung. When the United Nations troops drove the communists north, these men were killed together with many Protestants, Roman Catholics and such non-Christians as were considered to be against the communist government.

Han himself was arrested on June 30, 1950, just five days after the outbreak of war, with seven or eight other Christians. Among them was Rev Cho Huiyum and Elder Kim Choongsoon. They were held in a crowded prison through the hot summer months of 1950. In October, after MacArthur's Inchon landing on the west coast, word came that American troops had landed in Changjun Bay on the east coast. The prison guards became more watchful and strict.

It was estimated that there were between 700 and 800 prisoners in the jail at that time. Before retreating, the communists decided to kill off these prisoners. On the 7th October they started by tying rocks to them and drowning them at night, but so many corpses floated that they seemed to reject this method and in its place decided to take the prisoners into a tunnel dug into the hills behind the prison and shoot them.

Han was led from his cell at about seven o'clock on the evening of the 8th. On a table in the guard room were great boxes full of hemp cords in two-yard lengths as though prepared long in advance for this contingency. His hands were tied behind his back and then he was tied to three other prisoners, four abreast. Prisoners who had been tied up earlier were being moved out into the night. Han thought they were merely being moved to another location and did not suspect that their execution was in view. At about three or four in the morning of the 9th he and those tied with him were ordered to march. Guards were spaced at intervals up the hillside to the trench leading to the tunnel. As the prisoners stumbled up the hillside the guards would shout back acknowledging the arrival of one quartette and then call to the guard ahead that they were being passed along. It was not until Han entered the tunnel itself that he realized he was to face execution.

At the far end of the tunnel he could see corpses, tied in fours, piled three deep. In front of them was a communist soldier holding a pan of oil in which a light burned and beside him was another soldier with an automatic rifle. Han was so shocked at the sudden realization that he was about to die, that he felt he hardly had time to pray. He did not ask to have his life spared but prayed for God to protect his 83-year-old father and 4-year-old son and the little church which he had served, and then asked God to forgive him if he had hurt anyone with unkind words. The four were ordered to kneel on top of the three-deep pile of corpses, some still moving in death spasms. But Han had a bad leg and could not kneel easily, so sprawled on them with his legs sticking out behind him. The soldier with the automatic rifle started at the left, seizing each person by the collar and shooting him in the back of the head. He could see the face of the first man go down, then the head of the doctor to his left seemed to explode like a bowl. It was now his turn. But at that moment a head among the 'dead' in front of them was lifted and the man with the light said 'Get that black head.' The soldier stood on Han's back and fired at the man who had lifted his head. Then, evidently having forgotten he had not shot Han, while at the same time Han's sprawled posture made him look like one of the dead, he went on and shot the fourth man, leaving Han unscathed.

A fifth quartette was marched in and made to get on the pile on top of Han. It was then that, Han said, he had time to give way to fear. Having escaped the direct shot, he feared that the bullet for the man above him might pass through, and reach its mark in him. But he was spared. That section of the tunnel was now boarded up. Then he could hear the march of prisoners continue as they came into the tunnel to be shot. Some, sensing what they were facing, came in boldly singing battle songs to strengthen their courage. Last of all he could hear women being brought in, crying as they came. The guards on the outside called to them to speed up their work. When all 305 had been 'dispatched', he could hear the guards preparing to set off dynamite to close the mouth of the tunnel, and

[157]

jokingly warning one another to be careful not to share burial with the dead. Han wondered how men could be so callous as to joke at a time like this. The explosion sealed the mouth of the tunnel, but in the providence of God, the tunnel itself did not cave in, only small amounts of loose dirt fell from the ceiling. Again, providentially, two days later bombs from American aircraft opened a hole in the top of the tunnel. Two high school students, a girl, a farmer, and a doctor, and one other besides Han, survived the mass slaughter. Even after the hole was opened the survivors were afraid to come out as communists were still lurking in the area. One of the students who ventured forth has not been heard from since.

Eventually the United Nations troops came. Two hundred and ninety-eight bodies were found in this tunnel. Among them Han identified the above-mentioned minister, Cho Huiyum, and two Roman Catholic priests, but recognized no others. Truly, 'a thousand shall fall at thy side and ten thousand at thy right hand, but it shall not come nigh thee', without the Heavenly Father willing it.

It is but right to add that, in the changing fortunes of war, when an area was occupied by the United Nations troops, sometimes it was elders and church leaders who pointed out those among the populace who had worked for the communists, and helped to have them caught and executed. When such an area was retaken by the communists, reprisals against the Christians were rather to be expected. Where Christians had been generous with communists when territory changed hands, there were cases of communists being lenient with Christians. It must be remembered that many had been forced into the communist camp in order to survive, who were by no means communists at heart. There were cases in which Christians erred in not recognizing this distinction, thus occasioning ill-will against themselves.

It is important that, however devilish communism may be, we should not forget that the people through which it works are human beings, some of whom may even prove to be the subjects of God's electing grace and regenerating power. God's Word assures us that Satan and his forces will not prevail, for the saints 'overcame him because of the blood of the Lamb, and because of the word of their testimony; and they loved not their life even unto death' (Rev. 12:11).

In Part 2 of this small book, I have given only a few examples of the sufferings endured by the Korean Christians. The cases of those whose sufferings and martyrdoms have been recorded here, have passed into a history that goes back 25 years to the Korean War and beyond. But with its roots in such a beginning and in the midst of such testing suffering, the church grows on.

During the period recorded in the two parts of this book the Protestant Church in Korea has grown from the first believer, baptized in 1886, just 90 years ago, to the present 2,689,918 members worshipping in 1,304 churches throughout South Korea. This growth, in other words, has taken place during the life time of some people, Koreans, as well as Westerners, who are still living today.

The religious and even the secular press and the radio tell of the phenomenal growth and numbers of the churches in Korea. Public attention has been called to this little country, where one Christian gathering, three years ago, attracted over a million people, and in the following year another such gathering attracted one million five hundred thousand people, declared by some to be the largest Christian gatherings in the history of the Christian Church.

Since the baptism of that first Christian, 90 years ago, the Korean church has survived five wars. During this time the country has constantly seen foreign troops on her soil, or has been actually occupied in part or in whole by foreign nations, and now, finally, is governed by opposing political regimes.

Today the country is divided, not by the choice of the majority of the Korean people, but as the result of an agreement made between the leaders of China, Russia, Great Britain and the United States at Yalta, before the end of the Second World War. As a result of this agreement, since 1945 an atheistic Communist government has been ruling that half of the country north of the 38th parallel. It was in this northern half of the country that the church originally began, and grew strongest. It is the area in which most of the incidents recorded in both parts of this book took place.

After the Communists came into power in the northern half of Korea, thousands of Christians in that area, especially Christian ministers, church officers and leaders, were killed by them. During the Korean War, when the Communist armies over-ran all but the 50 mile Pusan perimeter, many Christians in South Korea were also killed by the Communist forces.

Before the 'bamboo curtain' became an 'iron wall', at the end of the Korean war, many thousands of Christians were able to escape south with the masses moving to flee from Communism, and contributed to the phenomenal population increase in the southern part of Korea of which we hear so much today.

Statistics and information about the church in the northern half of the country, where the revival took place, are not available today. But we know that the story is not finished and will not be until Jesus comes. While numerically the church in the southern half of Korea continues to grow in a remarkable way, there are many divisions and it has many adversaries. Korea's very openness to the Gospel has been the occasion of many cults springing up from within, as well as others coming from outside the country, causing the church to be, in the words of a familiar hymn,

> *By schisms rent asunder*
> *By heresies distressed*

Nevertheless we also know that *saints their watch are keeping*! May the story of the roots of the Korean church, and the sufferings which it has survived, point the reader to the Lamb of God who alone takes away the sin of the world.

We believe that the Lord has built this church, and for that reason the gates of hell will not prevail against it. May its story be an encouragement to all those who are working in the building of his kingdom, and may this account cause God's people everywhere to be in prayer for one another, especially for those who are going through times of testing.

Even so come, Lord Jesus